Contents

CHEESE DANISH

Prep Time: 20 minutes

Cooking Time: 1 hour & 20 minutes

Servings: 9 persons

INGREDIENTS

- 1 large egg yolk
- 8 ounces cream cheese
- 1 batch Danish dough
- 1 ¼ cup confectioners' sugar
- ½ teaspoon pure vanilla extract
- 1 large egg, lightly beaten
- 2 tablespoons/30 milliliters whole milk
- A pinch of salt

For Danish Dough:

- 2 tablespoons granulated sugar
- 1 ½ cups bread flour, plus more for the work surface and the rolling pin
- 14 tablespoons cold, unsalted butter, roughly cubed
- ¼ cup cold whole milk
- 1 large egg
- 2 teaspoons active dry yeast
- ¾ teaspoon kosher salt

DIRECTIONS

1. Beat the cream cheese with egg yolk, ¼ cup confectioners' sugar, vanilla and salt in a large-sized mixing bowl until completely smooth. Transfer the prepared mixture into a resealable plastic bag & set aside until ready to use.

2. Roll the dough out on a lightly floured surface into a 12 ½" square. Trim ¼" off each edge and then, cut the dough into nine 4" squares. Brush the corners of each square using the beaten egg and then fold each corner into the middle; gently press it down. Transfer the squares to 2 baking sheets lined with parchment.

3. Cut the tip off one corner of the filled plastic bag (approximately ½" hole). Use the bag to pipe the cheese filling onto the center of dough square. Using a plastic wrap; loosely cover the pastries & let stand for an hour or two, until slightly puffed. Preheat your oven to 425 F.

4. Remove the plastic wrap & gently brush the sides and top of your dough with the beaten egg. Bake in the preheated oven for 10 minutes, then rotate the sheets; decrease your oven's temperature to 375 F. Continue baking for 6 to 8 more minutes, until pastries turn deep golden brown and are puffed.

5. In the meantime, whisk the leftover confectioners' sugar with the milk. Let the Danish to slightly cool on the sheet and then, drizzle with the glaze. Serve warm or at room temperature & enjoy.

For Danish Dough:

1. Combine flour with yeast, granulated sugar & salt in the bowl of a food processor. Add butter & continue to pulse until combined well. Transfer the mixture to a medium-sized mixing bowl.

2. Whisk the egg with milk & 2 tablespoons of water in a small-sized bowl.

3. Add the prepared egg mixture into the flour mixture. Fold the mixture using a rubber spatula until moistened evenly. Turn the dough out onto a piece of plastic wrap & shape into a small rectangle; wrap well. Let chill for 3 hours.

4. Next, roll the dough out to an 8x15" rectangle using a floured rolling pin on a lightly floured surface. With a short side facing you, fold the dough in thirds like a letter, bringing the top third of the dough down, then folding the bottom third up. Use a bench scraper to help lift and fold the dough if required.

5. Rotate the dough 90 degrees. Repeat the rolling & folding process, then rotate the dough one more time & roll and fold again. As you work, dust the work surface, your hands and the rolling pin with flour as necessary. Wrap the dough in plastic wrap and refrigerate for an hour.

6. Repeat the entire rolling and folding process one more time for a grand total of six turns. If the dough starts to fight you and become difficult to roll at any point, just pop it in the fridge for an extra rest. Wrap the dough and refrigerate for at least 2 hours, or overnight

SWEET NUT PASTRY

Prep Time: 1 hour & 20 minutes

Cooking Time: 2 hours & 20 minutes

Servings: 12 persons

INGREDIENTS

For the Dough

- ¼ cup sugar
- 1 ½ ounces fresh yeast
- ⅓ cup melted butter
- 4 ½ cups bread flour plus more for dusting
- ¾ cup lukewarm milk
- 1 egg yolk, large
- A pinch of salt

For the Topping

- ¼ cup cream (approximately 38% fat)
- 5 ounces honey
- 1 ¾ cups pecan, chopped

- ½ cup light brown sugar

DIRECTIONS

1. Lightly grease an 11x12" cake tin with butter then, dissolve the yeast in ¼ cup of milk.
2. Combine the flour with sugar & salt in a large-sized mixing bowl & make a well in the center. Pour the prepared yeast mixture into the well; dust with a small amount of flour. Using a cloth; cover & let rise for 12 to 15 minutes.
3. Add the egg yolk, butter and leftover milk; mix well & knead until you get smooth dough like consistency. Shape the dough into a ball; add it to the mixing bowl again & cover with a cloth; let rise in a warm place until almost doubled in size, for an hour.
4. Next, heat the cream with honey, and brown sugar over moderate heat in a small pan; bring the mixture to a boil for a couple of minutes.
5. Sprinkle the nuts into the cake tin & then, drizzle with the caramel-honey mixture.
6. Preheat your oven to 400 F.
7. Turn the dough out onto a well-floured board, lightly knead and then evenly divide into 12 pieces. Shape these into balls & place them in the cake tin over the honey and nuts. Let rise for 12 to 15 more minutes.
8. Bake in the preheated oven until cooked through, for 40 to 50 minutes. Cool in the tin for a couple of minutes and then, place them on a wire rack to completely cool. Serve & enjoy.

APPLE FARM CINNAMON BUNS

Prep Time: 2 hours & 10 minutes

Cooking Time: 20 minutes

Servings: 12 persons

INGREDIENTS

For Dough:

- 1 tablespoon instant dry yeast
- 3 cups all-purpose flour
- 1 cup warm milk
- 3 tablespoons salted butter softened
- 1 large egg
- 2 tablespoons white granulated sugar
- 1 teaspoon salt

For Filling:

- ½ cup melted salted butter
- 2 tablespoons ground cinnamon
- 1 cup brown sugar

For Glaze:

- 4 ounces softened cream cheese
- ½ teaspoon vanilla extract
- 1 to 1 ½ cups powdered sugar
- ¼ cup softened butter, salted
- 1 to 2 tablespoons milk

DIRECTIONS

1. Combine the warm milk with sugar, yeast, eggs, butter, and salt in the bowl of a stand mixer. Add the flour & mix on a low speed, using a dough hook.
2. Once the flour begins to incorporate into the dough, slowly increase the speed to medium. Add more of flour as required so that the dough pulls away from the sides of your bowl. Ensure that the dough mixture is soft & tacky and not sticky. Feel free to add more of flour until you get your consistency of dough.
3. Transfer the prepared dough to a mixing bowl, lightly greased. Cover with a kitchen towel & let rise for an hour, until almost double in size.
4. Lightly grease a large-sized baking sheet; punching the dough down & roll into a 12x18" rectangle.
5. Brush the dough with approximately ½ cup of the melted butter. Combine the cinnamon with brown sugar in a small-sized mixing bowl. Sprinkle the mixture over the melted butter. Tightly roll up lengthwise until you get a long roll. Cut the dough into 12 1" slices using a sharp knife or plain dental floss.
6. Place the slices onto a lightly 9×13" pan. Cover & let rise for half an hour.
7. Preheat your oven to 325 F. Bake the rolls in the preheated oven until the top just turns brown, for 12 to 14 minutes.
8. In the meantime, prepare the cream cheese glaze. Whip the cream cheese with butter in a large bowl using a hand mixer until light & fluffy. Whip in the vanilla extract and powdered sugar. Add enough of milk until you get drizzle-like consistency. Frost the rolls while still warm. Serve immediately & enjoy.

CHRISTMAS PEPPERMINT DREAM CAKE

Prep Time: 35 minutes

Cooking Time: 1 hour & 15 minutes

Servings: 12 persons

INGREDIENTS

- 1 ½ cups all-purpose flour
- 3 organic eggs, large, at room temperature
- 1 ½ cups sugar

- ¾ cup milk

- 1 ½ teaspoons baking powder

- 3 tablespoons butter

- ½ teaspoon peppermint extract

- White chocolate curls

- 1 tablespoon liquid red food coloring

- Peppermint candy canes, chopped

- ¼ teaspoon salt

- 1 recipe Fluffy White Chocolate Frosting

DIRECTIONS

1. Lightly grease the bottoms of 2 round baking pans (8" each). Line the bottoms of pans with some waxed paper; grease & lightly flour the pans; set aside. Stir the flour with baking powder & salt in a small-sized mixing bowl; set the mixture aside until ready to use.

2. Preheat your oven to 350 F. Beat the eggs using an electric mixer in a medium-sized mixing bowl until thick & lemon colored, for a couple of minutes, on high speed. Slowly add the sugar; continue to beat until light & fluffy, for 4 to 5 minutes, on medium speed. Add the flour mixture; continue to beat until just combined, on low to medium speed.

3. Next, over medium heat in a small-sized saucepan; heat & stir the butter and milk until the butter is completely melted. Add the peppermint extract & milk mixture to the prepared batter; continue to beat until combined well. Evenly divide the batter in half. Pour ½ of the prepared batter into one of the baking pans. Stir red food coloring into the leftover batter. Pour the red batter into another baking pan.

4. Bake in the preheated oven until a wooden toothpick comes out clean, for 25 to 30 minutes. Let cool in pans on wire racks for several minutes. Remove the cakes from pans. Peel off the waxed paper & let completely cool on wire racks. Cut each cake layer horizontally into half.

5. To assemble, place a white cake layer on a serving plate. Evenly spread approximately ¾ cup of the frosting on top of the cake. Top with a red cake layer; evenly spread with ¾ cup of more frosting. Top with the leftover white cake layer; evenly spread with ¾ cup of frosting. Top with the red cake layer & evenly spread the leftover frosting on top & sides of your cake. Sprinkle the coarsely chopped candy canes and white chocolate curls over the cake. Cover & let chill for a couple of hours. Cover & store any remaining cake in the refrigerator.

BURSTING WITH BLUEBERRY CARDAMOM BUCKLE

Prep Time: 25 minutes
Cooking Time: 1 hour & 20 minutes

Servings: 8 persons

INGREDIENTS

- 2 cups blueberries, fresh
- 1 ½ cups all-purpose flour
- 2 organic eggs, large
- ½ teaspoon ground cardamom
- 2 teaspoons vanilla extract
- ¾ cup light brown sugar
- 2 teaspoons lemon zest, fresh
- ⅔ cup whole milk
- 2 teaspoons baking powder
- 1 stick salted butter (approximately ½ cup), melted

For Crumble:

- ¼ cup light brown sugar
- ½ cup all-purpose flour
- 4 tablespoons salted butter, at room temperature
- ½ teaspoon ground cinnamon

DIRECTIONS

1. Lightly coat a 9" spring form pan with butter and then, preheat your oven to 350 F.
2. Whisk the flour with baking powder, sugar, and cardamom in a large-sized mixing bowl. Add the milk, butter, vanilla, and eggs; continue to mix just until combined. Spoon the prepared batter into the pan. Toss the blueberries with lemon zest & sprinkle them on top of the batter in the pan.
3. For Crumble: Whisk the flour with cinnamon, and sugar in a small-sized mixing bowl. Add the butter & continue to mix using your hands until the crumble forms and mix is moist. Evenly sprinkle the prepared crumble on top of the fruit.
4. Bake in the preheated oven until the top turn golden and a skewer comes out almost clean, for 45 to 55 minutes. Let cool for a couple of minutes. Serve warm or at room temp; lightly dust with the powdered sugar. Enjoy.

CHOCOLATE OBLIVION CAKE

Prep Time: 2 hours

Cooking Time: 2 hours & 20 minutes

Servings: 24 persons

INGREDIENTS

- 2 ½ teaspoons instant espresso or coffee
- 1 ¼ teaspoon baking soda

- 8 organic eggs, large
- ¼ teaspoon baking powder
- 15 tablespoons butter
- 1 cup sour cream
- 12 ounces semisweet chocolate
- ½ cup butter
- 2 ½ teaspoon vanilla
- ¾ cup unsweetened cocoa
- 3 ¼ cups sugar
- 1 ½ cups whipping cream
- 2 cups cake flour
- A pinch of salt
- 3 ounces unsweetened chocolate

DIRECTIONS

1. Lightly grease 2 cake pans, (9" each) with butter and then, preheat your oven to 350 F.
2. Dissolve the espresso in 1 cup of hot water & let it cool.
3. Combine the flour with cocoa powder, 1 ½ cups of sugar, baking powder, baking soda & ¾ teaspoon of salt in a large-sized mixing bowl.
4. Add the espresso followed by 2 eggs, butter, sour cream & 1 teaspoon of vanilla; beat for a couple of minutes, on medium speed.
5. Pour the mixture into the greased pans. Bake for 25 to 30 minutes, until the cake pulls away from the sides of your pan. Let cool for 8 to 10 minutes on the racks and then, remove from the pans. Let completely cool.

For Chocolate Mousse:

1. Chop the unsweetened chocolate and 9 ounces of semisweet chocolate.
2. Over low heat; melt 12 tablespoons of butter. Once done; turn the heat off and stir in the chopped chocolate until completely smooth. Separate the leftover eggs.
3. Slowly beat ¾ cup of sugar into the yolks & beat in the chocolate mixture and 1 teaspoon of vanilla.
4. Continue to beat the egg whites with a pinch of salt until soft peaks form. Slowly beat in 6 tablespoons of sugar & continue to beat until stiff peaks form.
5. Gently fold the whites into the prepared chocolate mixture.
6. Beat ¾ cup of the cream until stiff and then, fold into the prepared chocolate mixture. Set 4 cups of this mousse aside until ready to use; refrigerate the leftover mousse.

For Assembling:

1. Make 4 thin layers of the cakes by cutting them horizontally into half.
2. Put two layers on separate plates. Spread each with approximately 2 cups of kept-aside mousse. Let chill for 20 minutes, until firm.

3. Top each with a second cake layer & refrigerate.

4. Beat the leftover ¼ cup of cream with vanilla and ¼ cup of sugar until stiff. Evenly spread the whipped cream on top of one of the layered cakes. Let chill for 25 to 30 minutes, until firm.

5. Top with the second layer of cake & let chill for 15 to 20 more minutes, until firm. Stir the leftover mousse to soften & evenly spread on top & sides of your cake.

6. Next, over low heat; melt the leftover butter with 3 ounces of semisweet chocolate.

7. Drizzle the mixture on top & around the edges of your cake. Serve and enjoy.

CRUMB CAKE GALORE

Prep Time: 25 minutes

Cooking Time: 55 minutes

Servings: 9 persons

INGREDIENTS

For Cake

- ¾ teaspoon baking powder
- 1 cup all-purpose flour
- ½ cup granulated sugar
- 5 tablespoons softened butter (2.5 ounces), unsalted
- ⅛ teaspoon baking soda
- 1 organic egg, large
- ¼ cup each of milk & sour cream (approximately 2 ounces each)
- 1 teaspoon vanilla extract
- ¼ teaspoon salt

For Crumbs

- ⅓ cup light brown sugar, packed
- 1 cup plus 2 tablespoons all-purpose flour
- ⅓ cup granulated sugar
- 1 teaspoon ground cinnamon
- ½ cup unsalted butter (approximately 4 ounces), melted
- ¼ teaspoon salt

DIRECTIONS

1. Lightly coat an 8x8" baking dish with butter; line with two sheets of parchment (coated with butter as well) and then, preheat your oven to 350 F.

For the Crumbs:

1. Whisk the brown sugar with cinnamon, granulated sugar and salt in a large-sized mixing bowl until mixed well. Pour in the melted butter; give the ingredients a good stir until combined well.

2. Slowly add the flour & continue to mix using a spatula or wooden spoon until no streaks of flour remain, for a couple of more minutes; set aside.

For the Cake:

1. Whisk the flour with baking soda, baking powder and salt in a separate large-sized mixing bowl for a couple of seconds; set aside.

2. Whip the butter with granulated sugar in the bowl of an electric stand mixer attached with the paddle attachment for a minute or two, until pale & fluffy. Mix in vanilla and egg. Whisk the milk with sour cream in a liquid measuring cup.

3. Add in ⅓ of the flour mixture into the butter mixture; continue to blend until just combined and then, add ½ of the milk mixture; continue to mix until just combined. Repeat the process for one more time and then end by mixing in last ⅓ of the flour mixture until almost combined; scrapping down the sides & bottom of your bowl using a rubber spatula & fold the batter until completely incorporated.

4. Pour the prepared batter into the baking dish & spread into an even layer; as you go, don't forget to break the crumb mixture into pea-sized crumbs & evenly drop on top of the batter.

5. Bake for 30 to 35 minutes, until a toothpick comes out clean. Let cool for 10 minutes in the cake pan and then lift the cake from pan using parchment overhang & let cool on a wire rack.

ULTIMATE CARROT CAKE WITH CARDAMOM

Prep Time: 50 minutes

Cooking Time: 50 minutes

Servings: 8 persons

INGREDIENTS

For Cake:

- 2 ½ cups plus 1 tablespoon unbleached all-purpose flour
- 1 ½ cups white sugar
- ½ cup crushed pineapple, drained
- 4 organic eggs, large, at room temperature
- ½ teaspoon ground cinnamon
- 3 cups carrots, grated (approximately 6 to 8 medium carrots)
- ½ cup light brown sugar, packed
- 1 ½ teaspoons baking powder
- ½ teaspoon baking soda
- 1 teaspoon ground cardamom
- ¾ cups pecans, toasted, chopped

- 1 cup buttermilk, at room temperature
- ¾ cup vegetable oil
- 2 teaspoons vanilla extract
- ½ teaspoon salt

For Icing:

- 1 cup almonds, sliced, toasted & coarsely chopped
- 4 ounces fine white chocolate, melted & cooled
- 6 cups sifted confectioners' sugar
- ¾ cup unsalted butter (approximately 1 ½ sticks), at room temperature
- 2 tablespoons heavy cream
- 1 ½ packages cream cheese (12 ounces), at room temperature
- 2 teaspoons vanilla extract

DIRECTIONS

For the Cake:

1. Lightly grease 3 round cake pans (8" each) & line the bottom of your pans with the parchment paper. Spray the pans and paper with the baking spray; set the pans aside and then, preheat your oven to 350 F.
2. Beat the sugars with oil in the bowl of an electric mixer until combined well, on medium speed. Mix in the vanilla & slowly add the eggs; mix well after each addition. Add the pineapple and carrots; continue to mix until combined well.
3. Sift the 2 ½ cups flour with baking soda, baking powder, cinnamon, cardamom and salt in a large-sized mixing bowl. With the mixer speed still on low speed; add the flour mixture into the prepared carrot mixture alternately with the buttermilk (starting & ending with the flour). Continue to mix until combined well. Toss the pecans with leftover flour in a small bowl. Fold the pecans into the prepared batter.
4. Evenly pour the formed batter into the cake pans. Bake for 35 to 45 minutes, until a toothpick comes out clean. Let the cakes to cool in the pans for 12 to 15 minutes on wire racks. Remove the cakes from pans & completely cool on the racks.
5. In the meantime, prepare the icing. Beat the cream cheese with butter in the bowl of an electric mixer until combined well, on medium speed. Decrease the speed to low & slowly add the confectioners' sugar; continue to mix until combined well. Add the white chocolate and vanilla. Increase the speed to medium-high & continue to beat for a minute or two, until completely smooth. Set 1 cup of icing aside for decoration. Add the heavy cream & beat until combined well.
6. For Frosting: Arrange a cake layer on a cake plate. Spread the top with the cream cheese icing and top with a second & third cake layer, evenly spreading the prepared icing between each layer. Spread the icing on top & around the sides of your cake. Apply the almonds to the sides of the frosted cake. Fill a pastry bag fitted with a star tip, with the kept-aside icing & pipe a border around the top of the cake. Cut the cake & serve.

DARK MOLASSES GINGERBREAD CAKE

Prep Time: 40 minutes

Cooking Time: 2 hours & 20 minutes

Servings: 10 persons

INGREDIENTS

- 1 ½ cups unsulphured blackstrap or unsulphured dark molasses (approximately 12 ounces)
- 2 ½ teaspoons baking soda
- ⅓ cup white sugar
- 3 ¼ cups all-purpose flour
- ¾ cup brown sugar
- 2 teaspoons espresso powder
- ½ teaspoon cinnamon
- 2 teaspoons ground ginger
- 1 teaspoon vanilla
- 2 beaten eggs, large
- 1 ½ cups whole milk
- 12 tablespoons unsalted butter, cut into chunks
- ½ teaspoon fine salt

For Icing:

- 1 cup whole milk
- 16 ounces full-fat cream cheese (2 bars), softened at room temperature for an hour
- 1 cup white sugar
- ¼ cup all-purpose flour
- 1 teaspoon vanilla
- ¼ teaspoon sugar

DIRECTIONS

1. Lightly grease or butter a 10" springform cake pan and then, preheat your oven to 350 F.

2. Place the butter chunks over medium heat in a 2 quarts saucepan. Add the molasses & whisk in the white and brown sugar; continue to whisk until the butter is completely melted and the sugar is no longer grainy and has dissolved; give the ingredients a good stir & turn the heat off; set aside at room temperature to cool.

3. Combine the flour with ginger, cinnamon, baking soda, espresso powder and salt, in a large-sized mixing bowl using a clean dry whisk.

4. Whisk the eggs, vanilla & milk with the molasses & melted butter into the saucepan. When combined

well; slowly pour the liquid into the bowl with the dry ingredients. Thoroughly whisk until combined well; ensure that there are no lumps remain.

5. Pour the thick batter into the prepared springform pan. Bake until a tester comes out clean, for 45 to 50 minutes. Let cool for half an hour and then, run a thin, flexible knife around the inside of your pan to help the cakes edges to release. Carefully remove the cake from pan & let completely cool on a cooling rack then, do the icing.

For Icing:

1. Place the cream cheese in the bowl of a stand mixer; whip until completely smooth & silky, for a couple of minutes, on high speed; scrapping out the cream cheese into a separate bowl & set aside.

2. Whisk the flour with sugar & salt over medium heat in a small saucepan. Slowly add the milk; continue to whisk until you get smooth paste like consistency. As the mixture comes up to a simmer; continue to whisk until thicken. Let simmer for a minute and then turn off the heat; scrapping the milk-flour paste into the mixer bowl.

3. Turn on the beaters or mixer & whip the milk-flour mixture until lightened & no longer piping hot, for 10 minutes. Slowly add the softened, whipped cream cheese; continue to whip. Add the vanilla & continue to whip until the two are combined completely, smooth & silky.

4. Refrigerate the icing until firms up. Briefly whip again on high speed before using.

SPICED DULCE DE LECHE BANANA ICEBOX CAKE

Prep Time: 20 minutes

Cooking Time: 6 hours & 10 minutes

Servings: 8 persons

INGREDIENTS

For the Icebox Cake:

- 6 ounces dulce de leche
- A pint of heavy whipping cream
- 1 box chocolate wafers
- 2 bananas, sliced
- 1 teaspoon vanilla
- ½ teaspoon salt

For the Spiced Dulce De Leche:

- 2 cans condensed milk, sweetened
- ½ teaspoon each of cinnamon & cardamom

DIRECTIONS

1. Thoroughly combine the milk with spices in a large-sized mixing bowl until combined well; pour the mixture into three canning jars, 8-ounce each. Secure the lids gently and then, put in a slow cooker; filling the slow cooker with hot water. Cook until milk has turned brown, on low-heat for 6 hours. Tighten the lids & put in a fridge.

For the Icebox Cake:

1. Whip the cream with salt and vanilla until stiff peaks just form. Drizzle in the dulce de leche; continue to mix until well incorporated. Layer the cookies followed by whipped cream & banana slices. Put the cake in the freezer until firm, let sit for 8 to 10 minutes on the counter before serving.

CARROT CAKE CUPCAKES

Prep Time: 20 minutes

Cooking Time: 20 minutes

Servings: 9 persons

INGREDIENTS

- ½ teaspoon baking soda
- 1 ½ cup white, spelt, or Bob's gf flour
- 2 tablespoons more sugar or 1/16 teaspoon uncut stevia
- ½ cup applesauce
- 1 teaspoon cinnamon
- ⅓ cup unrefined sugar or xylitol
- 2 teaspoons white or apple cider vinegar
- ½ cup raisins, optional
- 2 teaspoons pure vanilla extract
- ⅓ cup oil
- 1 packed cup carrot, shredded
- ¾ teaspoon salt

DIRECTIONS

1. Place 9 cupcake liners in a muffin tin and then, preheat your oven to 350 F.
2. Combine the entire dry ingredients together in a large-sized mixing bowl; mix well & set aside.
3. Combine the entire liquid ingredients together in a large measuring cup. Mix wet ingredients into the dry; immediately portion into the baking cups & bake for 17 to 20 minutes; let cool.
4. Once done; top them with your favorite frosting recipe and enjoy.

PEANUT BUTTER CUPCAKES

Prep Time: 20 minutes

Cooking Time: 25 minutes

Servings: 14 persons

INGREDIENTS

- ¾ cup whole milk, at room temperature
- 1 ¼ cups all-purpose flour
- ½ cup creamy peanut butter
- ⅓ cup sour cream, at room temperature
- 1 cup dark or light brown sugar, packed
- ½ teaspoon baking soda
- 1 ½ teaspoons pure vanilla extract
- ⅓ cup peanuts, very finely chopped or crushed
- ½ cup vegetable or canola oil
- 1 large egg, at room temperature
- ¼ teaspoon salt

For Chocolate Peanut Butter Frosting

- 3 tablespoons heavy cream or milk
- ½ cup Dutch-process or natural unsweetened cocoa powder
- 3 ½ cups confectioners' sugar
- 1 cup unsalted butter, softened, at room temperature
- ⅓ cup creamy peanut butter
- 1 teaspoon pure vanilla extract
- ¼ teaspoon salt

For Garnish, Optional:

- Mini Reese's peanut butter cups or chopped peanuts

DIRECTIONS

1. Preheat your oven to 350 F. Line a standard-sized muffin pan (12 cups) with cupcake liners. Line a second pan with 2 more liners; set aside.
2. For Cupcakes: Whisk the flour with baking soda & salt in a medium-sized mixing bowl; set the mixture aside.
3. Combine the oil with sour cream, peanut butter, egg, brown sugar, and vanilla extract using a stand or handheld mixer fitted with a paddle or whisk attachment, or a whisk in a large bowl. Add the dry ingredients, peanuts, and milk; beat or whisk until combined well and you get slightly thick batter like consistency. Ensure that you don't over mix the ingredients.
4. Spoon or pour the prepared mixture into the liners; filling them approximately ⅔ full. Bake in the preheated oven until a toothpick comes out clean, for 20 to 22 minutes. Let completely cool before you begin the frosting process.

5. For Frosting: Beat the butter with a stand or handheld mixer attached with a whisk or paddle attachment for 2 minutes, until creamy, on medium speed. Add the cocoa powder, confectioners' sugar & milk; continue to beat for 30 more seconds, on low speed and then, add the vanilla extract, peanut butter & salt. Beat until combined well, for 2 more minutes, on medium-high speed. Add approximately 1 to 2 tablespoons of more milk or cream; if the frosting appears to be too thick or ¼ cup of more confectioners' sugar if frosting appears to be too thin. Taste & add more of peanut butter or a pinch of salt, if required.

6. Frost the cooled cupcakes using Ateco 849 piping tip. Garnish with peanut butter cup, if desired.

7. Cover & store the leftovers in a refrigerator for up to 5 days.

BANANA SPLIT CHIFFON CAKE

Prep Time: 25 minutes

Cooking Time: 2 hours & 20 minutes

Servings: 8 persons

INGREDIENTS

For the Cake:

- 7 eggs, separated, at room temperature
- 1 ¼ teaspoon cream of tartar
- 2 large, overripe bananas, peeled & broken into rough chunks
- 1 cup plus ¼ cup sugar
- 2 tablespoons lemon juice, freshly squeezed
- 1 teaspoon vanilla extract
- 2 ¼ cups gluten-free flour
- ½ cup canola oil
- 2 teaspoons baking powder
- ½ teaspoon salt

For the Whipped Cream Frosting:

- 3 tablespoons sugar, powdered
- 1 ½ cups heavy cream

For the Filling:

- ½ cup heavy cream
- ⅓ cup cocoa powder
- ½ cup powdered sugar

DIRECTIONS

1. For easy cake removal; line three round baking pans, 8″ with aluminum foil; set them aside and then, preheat your oven to 325 F.

2. Blend the bananas with lemon juice & oil in a food processor or blender until completely smooth; stopping & scraping as required.

3. Slowly add the vanilla and egg yolks; continue to blend for a couple of more seconds, until combined well.

4. Next, combine flour with baking powder, 1 cup sugar & salt in the bowl of a stand mixer attached with the whisk attachment for 30 seconds, on low speed.

5. Make a well in the middle & pour in the prepared banana mixture.

6. Continue to beat until the entire dry ingredients are moistened, on low speed, scraping down the sides of your bowl as required.

7. Increase the speed to medium-high & beat for a minute or two, until completely smooth.

8. Next, whip the cream of tartar with egg whites in the mixer bowl attached with the whisk attachment until foamy, on medium-low speed.

9. Increase the speed to medium-high & continue to beat for a minute more, until soft peaks form.

10. Slowly add ¼ cup of sugar & beat until mixture is stiff & glossy.

11. Add a large scoop of the whipped egg whites into the prepared banana mixture & gently mix until the batter is lightened.

12. Work in batches and add the leftover egg whites. Using a large wire whisk; gently fold into the batter; ensure that you scrape down the bottom of your bowl every now and then.

13. Evenly divide the batter between the prepared pans.

14. Bake in the preheated oven for 25 minutes. Once done; increase the heat to 350 F & continue to bake until a toothpick comes out clean, for 12 to 15 more minutes.

15. Once done; let the cake to rest & cool down a bit then, carefully remove the cakes from your oven

16. Carefully unmold the cakes.

17. Next, prepare the whipped cream using the mixer with the whisk attachment. Beat 3 tablespoons of powdered sugar with 1 ½ cups of heavy cream until whipped cream holds stiff peaks, on medium speed; scrapping the mixture into a clean bowl.

18. Without cleaning the whisk attachment or the mixing bowl; beat ½ cup of heavy cream with cocoa powder & ½ cup of powdered sugar until mixed well and fluffy.

19. Place one cake layer on a large-sized serving plate; spread with ½ of the prepared filling. Top with the second layer & spread with the remaining filling. Feel free to use your fingers for this step.

20. Top with the third layer. Frost the sides & then the top of your cake using the whipped cream.

21. Refrigerate the cake until ready to serve.

STRAWBERRY FRAISIER

Prep Time: 20 minutes

Cooking Time: 1 hour & 20 minutes

Servings: 4 persons

INGREDIENTS

For Biscuit Base

- 3 tablespoons butter
- 100g shortbread

For Elderflower Mousse

- 400ml of double cream
- 2 large egg yolks
- 15g of cornflower
- 2 tablespoons sugar
- 3 tablespoons of elderflower cordial
- 1 cup milk
- 2g of platinum grade gelatin leaves, (approx. 2 leaves)

For Decoration:

- ½ pound strawberries, small, halved

For Strawberry Jelly:

- 1 cup strawberries, halved
- ½ gelatin leaf
- 1 tablespoon sugar

DIRECTIONS

1. For Biscuit Base: Place the biscuits in a large-sized bowl & crush them using a rolling pin until you get fine sand consistency like mixture, for a couple of seconds. Melt the butter & stir into the crushed biscuits until incorporated well.

2. Line a small tray with greaseproof paper and place the food rings on it. Evenly divide the prepared biscuit mixture into four; gently pressing them down (in an even layer) into the base of food rings. Place the tray in the freezer until ready to use and you prepare the mousse

3. For the elderflower mousse: Start the process by soaking the gelatin in ice-cold water. Next, over moderate heat in a small saucepan; heat the milk until boiling; turn off the heat.

4. In the meantime, whisk the egg yolks with cornflower, sugar and elderflower cordial in a small-sized mixing bowl. Remove the milk from the boil & slowly whisk it into the egg yolk mixture until completely incorporated

5. Sieve the mixture into the saucepan again & continue to heat for a couple of more minutes, until thickened, stirring constantly. Squeeze the gelatin leaves out & thoroughly whisk them into the hot custard. Set aside for a couple of minutes to cool down a bit.

6. Remove the frozen biscuit bases from freezer & place a layer of strawberries (cut-side facing outwards) carefully around the inside edge of each ring mold

7. Whisk the double cream in a large bowl until soft peaks form. Take a spoonful of the cream &

thoroughly combine it with the custard and then, gently fold the leftover double cream through the custard until it's smoothly incorporated; ensure that you don't knock the entire air out of your double cream

8. Gently spoon the mousse into each ring mold inside the strawberries and then smooth the mousse carefully over the top of them to fill the ring mold; leaving a minimum of 2mm of space at the top. Place the ring molds back into the freezer and let chill.

9. For Strawberry Jelly: Place the halved strawberries with the sugar over low heat in a small saucepan; give the ingredients a good stir and continue to cook until the sugar is completely dissolved, for 2 minutes. Cover & cook until the strawberries have released all their juice, for 10 minutes, don't stir the ingredients. Just 5 minutes before the strawberries are ready; place ½ of a gelatin leaf into the cold water

10. Strain the strawberries into a jug using a sieve; ensure that you don't push the strawberries too much. Place the strawberry juice into the pan again & continue to heat for a minute more. Squeeze the gelatin leaf out & stir it into the hot strawberry juice until thoroughly incorporated; leaving the strawberry juice to cool down to room temperature before pouring a thin layer over each of the chilled elderflower mousses. Place the mousses into the fridge & let chill for half an hour, until set.

11. To unmold the mousses; remove them from the fridge & gently run a blowtorch very quickly around the sides of the molds then pull the molds off. Decorate with the leftover strawberry halves & serve chilled.

CHOCOLATE BUTTER-CRUNCH TOFFEE

Prep Time: 10 minutes
Cooking Time: 10 minutes
Servings: 24 persons

INGREDIENTS

- 1 teaspoon espresso powder
- 1 ½ cups sugar
- 1 cup unsalted butter
- 3 tablespoons water
- 1 tablespoon light corn syrup
- 2 cups slivered almonds or pecans, diced, toasted
- 1 teaspoon baking soda
- 2 ⅔ cups chocolate chips; or bittersweet or semisweet chocolate, finely chopped
- ½ teaspoon salt

DIRECTIONS

1. Over moderate heat in a deep, large saucepan; heat the butter until melted. Once done; stir in the

espresso powder, corn syrup, sugar, water and salt; give the ingredients a good stir and bring the mixture to a boil. Let gently boil over medium heat for 10 to 12 minutes, until the mixture reaches hard-crack stage, don't stir the ingredients at this time. Keep an eye on the mixture; don't let it burn.

2. In the meantime, spread half of the nuts on a 9x13" pan lined with parchment in an even, closely packed layer. Top the nuts with half of the chocolate.

3. Remove the syrup from the heat; when it reaches 295 F & then, carefully stir in the baking soda. Quickly pour the prepared syrup evenly on top of the chocolate and nuts. Top with the leftover chocolate; let sit until softens, for 2 to 3 minutes. Next, using an offset spatula; spread the chocolate in an even layer & immediately sprinkle with the leftover nuts.

4. Pull the candy out of the pan; while it's still slightly warm & loosen it from the parchment using a thin spatula. When cool completely, break into uneven chunks.

5. Tightly wrap the cooled candy & store at room temperature for a couple of weeks or freeze for longer storage.

BOURBON PECAN BUTTER BALLS

Prep Time: 25 minutes

Cooking Time: 45 minutes

Servings: 3 ½ dozen

INGREDIENTS

For Buttery Toasted Pecans:

- ½ teaspoon ground red pepper
- 4 cups pecan halves
- ¼ cup butter, melted
- 1 teaspoon kosher salt

For Bourbon Balls

- 1 package vanilla wafers (12-ounces), finely crushed
- ½ cup bourbon
- 1 cup powdered sugar
- 2 tablespoons light corn syrup
- 1 cup toasted pecans, finely chopped
- 2 tablespoons unsweetened cocoa
- Powdered sugar, for coating

DIRECTIONS

For Buttery Toasted Pecans:

1. Preheat your oven to 325 F. Toss the pecans with butter in a large-sized mixing bowl.

2. Spread pecans in a jelly-roll pan in a single layer & bake in the preheated oven until toasted & turn

fragrant, for 20 to 25 minutes, stirring halfway during the baking process.

3. Remove them from the oven & sprinkle with pepper and salt; gently toss to coat. Let completely cool &
    then, store them for up to one week.

For Bourbon Balls:

1. Stir the entire ingredients (except the powdered sugar) together and then, make 1" balls from the
    prepared mixture. Roll each ball into the coarsely chopped Buttery Toasted Pecans or powdered sugar.
    Refrigerate for up to 2 weeks.

PEPPERMINT CHIP MERINGUE

Prep Time: 20 minutes

Cooking Time: 2 hours & 20 minutes

Servings: 1 ½ dozen

INGREDIENTS

- 2 large egg whites, room temperature
- ⅛ teaspoon salt
- ⅛ teaspoon cream of tartar
- ½ cup sugar
- 2 peppermint candy canes, crushed

DIRECTIONS

1. Beat the egg whites in a large-sized mixing bowl until foamy, for a couple of minutes and then, sprinkle
    with the cream of tartar & salt; continue to beat for a couple of more minutes, until soft peaks form.
    Slowly add sugar; beating well for 5 to 7 minutes, until stiff peaks form. Using teaspoonfuls; drop the
    mixture onto baking sheets lined with paper or ungreased foil; sprinkle with the crushed candy.

2. Bake for 1 ½ hours, at 225 F. Turn off the heat; open the door of your oven and leave the cookies inside
    it for 1 hour, until cool. Store them in an airtight container.

NUTELLA TRUFFLES

Prep Time: 20 minutes

Cooking Time: 2 hours & 40 minutes

Servings: 30 persons

INGREDIENTS

- ½ cup chocolate hazelnut spread
- 14 ounces dark or semisweet chocolate
- 1 teaspoon canola or vegetable oil, optional
- ⅓ cup heavy cream

- Roasted hazelnuts, finely chopped, for sprinkling

DIRECTIONS

1. Line a large-sized baking sheet with wax paper & set aside until ready to use.

2. Place 10 ounces of the chocolate into a medium-sized mixing bowl. Heat the heavy cream in the microwave until hot (ensure that you don't bring it to a boil). Pour the hot cream on top of the chocolate & let stand for a couple of minutes.

3. Stir the mixture using a rubber spatula until chocolate is completely melted & combined. Stir in the chocolate hazelnut spread. Using a plastic wrap; cover & refrigerate until set, for 2 hours.

4. Scoop the chocolate mixture out & form into balls using a small cookie scoop. Place onto the prepared cookie sheet and then, place in the freezer for half an hour.

5. Heat the leftover chocolate in the microwave-safe bowl until melted completely. Add oil; give it a good stir until combined well. Remove the chocolate balls form freezer & slowly place into the melted chocolate, one ball at a time. Evenly coat each ball with the melted chocolate using a fork. Remove the truffle from the chocolate using a fork and slightly tap the fork against the side of the bowl to get rid of any excess chocolate then before transfer the balls over the baking sheet again.

6. Pour the remaining melted chocolate into a small zip top bag, cut off one corner & pipe the melted chocolate per your likings on top; finish the process with the hazelnuts.

7. Place the truffles into the fridge again and let chill until truffles are set, for 15 more minutes. Enjoy.

BUTTER PECAN CRUNCH

Prep Time: 20 minutes

Cooking Time: 2 hours & 10 minutes

Servings: 12 persons

INGREDIENTS

For Crust:

- 2 tablespoons sugar
- 10 graham crackers
- 7 tablespoons butter, melted
- 1 tablespoon brown sugar

For Filling:

- 2 heath candy bars
- 1-quart butter-pecan ice cream
- 2 boxes instant vanilla pudding
- 1 small tub cool whip
- 2 cups milk

DIRECTIONS

1. Prepare the graham cracker crust in the bottom of a 9x13" pan.
2. Next, combine the vanilla pudding with milk and then, add the butter-pecan ice cream.
3. Pour the mixture over the graham cracker crust and then put in a freezer until chill.
4. Just before you serve, top the crunch with 2 chopped up Heath candy bars & Cool Whip. Enjoy.

FLOURLESS CHOCOLATE COOKIE

Prep Time: 12 minutes

Cooking Time: 20 minutes

Servings: 12 persons

INGREDIENTS

- 1 or 2 egg whites, large, at room temperature
- ⅓ cup unsweetened cocoa powder
- 1 teaspoon vanilla extract
- 1 ½ cup powdered sugar
- ½ cup semi-sweet chocolate chips
- A pinch of salt

DIRECTIONS

1. Line a large-sized baking sheet with the parchment paper and then, preheat your oven to 355 F.
2. Whisk the cocoa powder with icing sugar & salt in a large-sized mixing bowl.
3. Add the egg white & vanilla extract; continue to whisk until you get thick, moist batter like consistency. Feel free to add more of egg white, if it seems to be too thick.
4. Fold in the chocolate chips.
5. Scoop the batter over the prepared baking sheet; ensure that they are evenly spread and there is some space among them.
6. Bake in the preheated oven until the tops turn glossy & start to crack, for 12 to 14 minutes.
7. Let the cookies to completely cool then, remove them from the baking sheet using a large spatula.
8. Store the flourless chocolate cookies for up to 3 days, at room temperature in an airtight container.

DOUBLE FUDGE COOKIE

Prep Time: 20 minutes

Cooking Time: 20 minutes

Servings: 16 persons

INGREDIENTS

- 2 cups all-purpose flour
- ¼ cup granulated sugar

- 2 sticks unsalted butter (approximately 1 cup)
- ¾ cup light brown sugar
- 2 organic eggs, large-sized
- 1 packet Hershey's Instant Chocolate pudding
- 2 cups mini chocolate chips
- ⅓ cup unsweetened cocoa powder
- 2 teaspoons vanilla extract
- 1 teaspoon baking soda

DIRECTIONS

1. Line a large-sized baking sheet with parchment paper or a Silpat and then, preheat your oven to 350 F.
2. Combine the butter with sugars, vanilla extract and eggs in the bowl of a stand mixer with the whisk attachment. Beat for a couple of minutes, until just blended, on medium speed.
3. Add the cocoa powder and pudding mix; continue to mix for a minute more, scraping the sides as required.
4. Add baking soda and flour; mix until just blended, for a minute or two, scraping the sides as required.
5. Remove the bowl from stand & fold in the chocolate chips using a large spatula.
6. Roll the batter by hand into balls (approximately ¼ cup for small or ½ cup size for large cookies) & arrange them on prepared baking pan. Bake in the preheated oven until edges are set & center still looks undercooked, 10 minutes for large cookies or 8 minutes for small.
7. Let cool on the pan for 10 minutes and then, carefully remove them to the cooling rack.
8. Store them in an airtight container for up to one week or freeze them for up to 4 months.

FLOURLESS PEANUT BUTTER COOKIE

Prep Time: 10 minute
Cooking Time: 10 minutes
Servings: 16 persons

INGREDIENTS

- 1 teaspoon pure vanilla extract
- 1 cup natural peanut butter
- 1 organic egg, large, lightly beaten
- 1 cup sugar
- Coarse sea salt, for sprinkling

DIRECTIONS

1. Place the racks in the upper & lower third of your oven and then, preheat it to 350 F.
2. Combine the peanut butter with vanilla, egg and sugar in a medium-sized mixing bowl until combined well. Spoon approximately 1 tablespoon of the prepared mixture onto ungreased baking sheets

(approximately an inch apart). Flatten the mounds with the tines of a fork, making a crosshatch pattern on the cookies and then, sprinkle the cookies with the coarse salt.

3. Bake in the preheated oven for 8 to 10 minutes, until the edges turn golden around, switching the position of the sheets halfway during the baking process. Transfer to wire racks to completely cool & repeat the process with the leftover dough.

LEMON BARS

Prep Time: 20 minutes

Cooking Time: 45 minutes

Servings: 20 persons

INGREDIENTS

- 2 sticks salted butter (approximately 1 cup), cut into small cubes
- ½ cup sugar
- 2 cups all-purpose flour
- ¼ teaspoon salt

For Filling

- 1 ½ cup sugar
- Juice & zest of 4 medium-sized lemons
- 4 whole large eggs
- ¼ cup flour
- Powdered sugar, for sifting

DIRECTIONS

1. For the crust: Lightly grease a 9x13" pan with some butter and then, preheat your oven to 350 F.
2. Stir the flour with sugar & salt. Add the butter to the bowl & cut it all together using a pastry cutter until the mixture resembles fine crumbs. Press into the prepared pan & bake in the preheated oven for 15 to 20 minutes, until the edges turn golden.
3. For Filling: Stir the flour with sugar. Crack in the eggs; whisk to combine. Add the lemon juice and zest; continue to mix until combined well. Pour the mixture on top of the crust & bake for 15 to 20 more minutes.
4. Let cool in the fridge for 2 hours and then, sift the powdered sugar on top then cut into squares

TUXEDO CAKE

Prep Time: 25 minutes

Cooking Time: 2 hours & 50 minutes

Servings: 8 persons

INGREDIENTS

For No-Bake Cheesecake Filling:

- 3 bricks cream cheese (8 ounces each), softened at room temperature
- ½ cup each: white chocolate chips, dark chocolate chips
- 2 teaspoons vanilla
- ¾ cup condensed milk, sweetened
- 1 ½ tablespoon unflavored gelatin
- Chopped caramels or chocolate
- ½ cup sour cream
- Caramel sauce
- 2-3 tablespoons water
- Chocolate syrup

For Chocolate Cake Layers:

- 1 ½ cups white granulated sugar
- 1 cup softened butter, at room temperature
- ½ cup dark cocoa powder
- 4 organic eggs, large
- 1 teaspoon vanilla extract
- 4 teaspoons baking powder
- 1 ½ cups all-purpose flour
- 1 cup milk
- ½ teaspoon salt

DIRECTIONS

1. For Chocolate Cake: Line a large-sized baking sheet, (12x19") with the parchment paper; lightly coat the sides with some nonstick spray and then, preheat your oven to 350 F.

2. Cream the butter with sugar in a large-sized mixing bowl. Add the vanilla extract and eggs; beat until light & fluffy, for a couple of minutes. Slowly pour the milk and continue to beat until incorporated well.

3. Combine the entire dry ingredients such as cocoa powder, flour, baking powder and salt together in a separate large-sized mixing bowl; mix well. Add the dry ingredients using a sifter & continue to mix until just combined; ensure that you don't over-mix.

4. Pour the prepared cake batter into the pan & evenly spread to the edges. Bake until a toothpick center comes out clean & the center is set, for 30 to 35 minutes. Remove the baked cake from oven; set aside and let cool at room temperature.

5. For Cheesecake Filling. Beat the cream cheese in a stand mixer bowl until light & fluffy, for 8 to 10 minutes; scrapping the sides of your bowl down, as required until the cream cheese is completely mixed.

6. Add the sweetened condensed milk, sour cream & vanilla. Continue to mix until the ingredients are combined well, for a couple of more minutes.

7. Place the chocolates into separate small-sized bowls & melt the chocolate using a microwave or double boiler until completely smooth; set aside.

8. For Gelatin. In a small-sized mixing bowl; dissolve the gelatin in water & then heat for a minute in the microwave, until gelatin is completely melted and smooth, stirring after every 10 seconds. Let the gelatin to bloom for a couple of minutes; if using sheet gelatin.

9. Next, temper the gelatin. Add a cup of the cheesecake filling into the gelatin; whisk until combined well. Add the prepared tempered gelatin into the leftover cheesecake filling. Continue to mix for a couple of minutes, on high speed; scrapping down the sides of your bowl, as required.

10. Work quickly & evenly divide the prepared cheesecake filling between the bowls with the melted chocolate. Fold each chocolate & filling together using a spatula.

11. Return to the cooled cake & cut 2 circles out; each 8" in diameter. Transfer one cake circle into a cake pan, or springform pan lined with plastic wrap.

12. Spread the chocolate cheesecake filling over cake layer. Drizzle with chocolate syrup and caramel sauce. Top with the second layer of cake then add the prepared white chocolate cheesecake mixture. Drizzle the top with some more chocolate and caramel.

13. Transfer the cake into a refrigerator and let chill until completely set. Garnish with some chopped caramels or chocolate.

CREAM CHEESE POUND CAKE

Prep Time: 20 minutes

Cooking Time: 1 hour & 20 minutes

Servings: 16 persons

INGREDIENTS

- 3 cups sugar
- 1 ½ cups softened butter, at room temperature
- 6 organic eggs, large, at room temp
- 1 package cream cheese (8 ounce), softened
- 3 cups all-purpose flour
- 1 ½ teaspoons vanilla (or use almond extract)
- 2 teaspoons salt

DIRECTIONS

1. Generously grease a 4 quarts tube pan or two 8 x 4" loaf pans and then, preheat your oven to 350 F.

2. Cream the cream cheese with butter in a large-sized mixing bowl until completely smooth.

3. Add sugar & beat for a couple of minutes, until light & fluffy.

4. Slowly add the eggs; ensure that you beat the mixture well after each addition and then, mix in the
    vanilla.

5. With the mixer still on low; add flour & salt in two additions then, immediately transfer the batter into
    the prepared pan.

6. Tap the pans and ensure that there are no air bubbles in the prepared batter.

7. Bake in the preheated oven until a toothpick comes out clean, for 60 to 75 minutes.

8. If the tops start to turn brown quickly then, tent loosely with aluminum foil.

9. Let cool in the pans for a couple of minutes.

10. Turn the cakes out and then, completely cool with the tops up on a wire rack.

CHOCOLATE PAVLOVA

Prep Time: 25 minutes

Cooking Time: 1 hour & 35 minutes

Servings: 8 persons

INGREDIENTS

- 6 large egg whites
- 1 square bittersweet chocolate (1 ounce), melted
- 3 tablespoons cocoa powder, unsweetened
- ¼ teaspoon cream of tartar
- 2 squares bittersweet chocolate (1 ounce each), melted
- 1 ½ cups granulated sugar
- 3 cups strawberries, fresh, hulled & halved
- 1 tablespoon vinegar
- 2 teaspoons cornstarch
- 1 ½ cups whipping cream
- 2 teaspoons granulated sugar
- ¼ teaspoon salt
- 2 teaspoons vanilla extract

DIRECTIONS

1. Preheat your oven to 275 F.

2. Beat the egg whites with cream of tartar & salt in a large-sized mixing bowl until soft peaks form. Work
    in batches & add approximately 3 tablespoons of sugar at a time; beat for a couple of more minutes,
    until stiff & glossy peaks form. Sift the cornstarch and cocoa over the egg whites; gently fold them in.
    Gently fold in the vanilla, vinegar & the melted chocolate.

3. Line a large-sized baking sheet with the parchment paper & then, spread the meringue into 8"circle.
    Bake in the middle rack until the center is soft & outside is crispy, for 1 ½ hours. Loosen the meringue

from the parchment paper using a metal spatula & remove on a wire rack to cool. Let completely cool.

4. Whip the cream with sugar & evenly spread on top of the meringue. Decorate your cake with the strawberries & drizzle with some chocolate.

NEW YEAR'S HONEY CAKE

Prep Time: 50 minutes

Cooking Time: 1 hour & 50 minutes

Servings: 10 persons

INGREDIENTS

For the Cake:

- 3 large eggs
- ¾ cup honey
- 4 Granny Smith apples; peeled, cored & shredded
- ¼ cup light brown sugar
- 1 ½ teaspoons vanilla
- 3 cups all-purpose baking flour
- 1 teaspoon baking soda
- ¼ teaspoon allspice
- 1 ½ teaspoons cinnamon
- ½ cup white sugar
- 1 teaspoon baking powder
- A dash of ground cloves
- 1 ¼ cups canola oil
- ¾ teaspoon salt

For the Icing:

- 1 cup plus 3 tablespoons powdered sugar
- 1-2 tablespoons non-dairy creamer
- ¼ teaspoon vanilla

DIRECTIONS

1. Preheat your oven to 325 F. Beat the eggs in a large-sized mixing bowl until frothy. Whisk in the brown sugar, white sugar, honey, vanilla and oil. Sift the flour with cinnamon, baking soda, baking powder, spices, and salt in a separate medium-sized mixing bowl. Incorporate the flour mixture into the liquid; give the ingredients a good stir until blended well and then, fold in the shredded Granny Smith apples

2. Lightly coat a Bundt pan with some cooking spray; ensure that you coat the inner surface completely. Pour the prepared batter into the pan; filling the pan approximately ¾ full or a little less. Gently push the batter to the outside of your pan using a spatula; slightly pushing up the walls. Smooth the batter on the

top until flat & even all the way around the pan

3. Bake until a toothpick comes out clean, for 75 to 90 minutes.

4. Once done; let cool for 10 minutes and then, invert it onto a flat plate; gently tapping the Bundt pan to release the cake. Feel free to use a plastic knife to loosen the cake carefully around the sides & center tube; if your cake sticks. Let the cake to completely cool before the frosting process.

5. It's essential for you to decorate the cake on the same day you plan to serve it. For easy cleanup; do this part on a wire cooling rack with a piece of parchment paper underneath to catch additional drips or sugar. Put 3 tablespoons of the powdered sugar into a sifter or handheld mesh strainer. For an even shower of sugar around the surface of your cake; sprinkle sugar over the cake by tapping the strainer.

6. Now, prepare the drizzle icing. Sift a cup of the powdered sugar into a large-sized mixing bowl. Add approximately 1 tablespoon of non-dairy creamer & ¼ teaspoon of vanilla extract to the bowl; give the ingredients a good stir using a fork or whisk until blended well. Using teaspoons; add the extra non-dairy creamer; continue to mix after each addition until the mixture has the texture of very thick honey, but still pourable. When you could drizzle the icing in stripes across the surface the texture is right

7. Place a Ziploc bag inside a large water glass, open end facing upward & wrapped around the edge of the glass, so there is an open space for easy filling. Pour the prepared icing into the Ziploc bag

8. Close the bag, leaving a small bit open to vent. Guide the icing towards one of the lower corners of the bag. Cut the very tip of that corner off the bag. Drizzle the icing in a zig-zag pattern around the cake by squeezing the Ziploc bag gently to release the glaze. Let the icing to completely dry before serving, for an hour. Slice and enjoy

LEMON ICEBOX CAKE

Prep Time: 20 minutes

Cooking Time: 4 hours & 20 minutes

Servings: 15 persons

INGREDIENTS

- 1 box graham crackers (16 ounces)
- 2 packages of lemon instant pudding mix (3.4 ounces)
- 1 tub whipped topping (16 ounces), thawed & divided
- 2 ½ cups milk

For Garnish, Optional:

- Fresh berries and/or graham cracker crumbles

DIRECTIONS

1. Whisk the milk with instant pudding mix in a large-sized mixing bowl for a couple of minutes and then, fold in ½ of the whipped topping.

2. Cover the bottom of a 9x13" baking dish with a single layer of graham crackers. Evenly spread half of

the pudding mixture into an even layer. Repeat with one more layer of the graham crackers; then, the leftover pudding. Top with a third layer of the graham crackers and then the leftover whipped topping.

3. Cover & refrigerate for overnight.

4. Garnish with the optional graham cracker crumbles and/or fresh berries. Slice into desired pieces; serve and enjoy.

STRAWBERRY SHORTCAKE

Prep Time: 20 minutes

Cooking Time: 45 minutes

Servings: 4 persons

INGREDIENTS

- 2 pints ripe, rinsed strawberries
- 4 cups all-purpose flour
- 1 ¼ cups butter
- 3 tablespoons sugar
- ¼ teaspoon vanilla extract
- 5 teaspoons baking powder
- ½ cup sugar or to taste
- 3 cups whipping cream
- ¼ teaspoon salt

DIRECTIONS

1. Pick over & hull the strawberries. Depending upon the size; feel free to slice them into pieces or cut into half. Gently crush ¼ of the strawberries using a fork until you get their juices. Mix with the leftover berries & ½ cup of sugar. Cover & set it aside for half an hour.

2. Preheat your oven to 450 F.

3. Sift the flour with 3 tablespoons sugar, baking powder and salt in a large-sized mixing bowl. Add approximately ¾ cup of the softened butter; rubbing into the dry ingredients. Add 1 ¼ cups of the cream; continue to mix until you get soft dough like consistency. Next, on a lightly floured pastry board; knead the dough for a minute and then, roll it to approximately ½" thickness; cut an even number of rounds - 2 rounds per serving using a 3" biscuit cutter.

4. Next, lightly grease a large-sized baking sheet with a small amount of butter. Place half the rounds on it. Melt the leftover butter & brush a little on the rounds; place the leftover rounds on top. Bake in the preheated oven until turn golden brown, for 10 to 15 minutes.

5. Remove from the oven; pull the shortcakes apart. Brush the insides with some of the leftover melted butter.

6. Beat the leftover cream until thickens; slowly add the vanilla & beat until just thick.

7. Place a bottom half of shortcake on each plate. Top with a generous spoonful of the berries. Cover with a top half, add a few more berries, & top with the whipped cream. Serve immediately & enjoy.

CHOCOLATE MOUSSE CAKE

Prep Time: 40 minutes

Cooking Time: 50 minutes

Servings: 16 persons

INGREDIENTS

For the Cake

- 3 ounces unsweetened chocolate, finely chopped
- ¾ cup granulated sugar
- 2 tablespoons Dutch-processed cocoa powder, unsweetened
- ½ cup buttermilk
- 6 tablespoons unsalted butter, softened
- 1 teaspoon vanilla extract
- ¼ cup hot water
- 2 large eggs
- ¾ teaspoon baking soda
- 2 large egg yolks
- ¾ cup all-purpose flour
- 1 teaspoon instant coffee granules
- ½ teaspoon salt

For the Mousse

- 2 tablespoons granulated sugar
- 1 ½ cups cold heavy cream
- 6 ounces semisweet chocolate, coarsely chopped
- 1 tablespoon water
- ¾ teaspoon gelatin powder

For the Ganache

- 9 ounces semisweet chocolate, coarsely chopped
- 1 tablespoon unsalted butter
- ¾ cups heavy cream

DIRECTIONS

For the Cake:

1. Lightly grease & flour an 8" springform pan; tap out any excess flour and then, arrange the rack in the

center position of your oven & preheat to 350 F.

2. Place the chocolate in a small-sized heatproof bowl. Fill a pot with water and bring it to a boil; pour the hot boiling water on top of the chocolate. Using a silicone spatula; give it a good stir for a couple of minutes, until the chocolate is completely melted & smooth. Stir in the cocoa powder and coffee granules. Add ¼ cup of sugar; give it a good stir for a minute or two, until thick & glossy.

3. Beat the butter & leftover sugar until light & fluffy in the bowl of a stand mixer attached with the paddle attachment. Slowly beat in the egg yolks & eggs; mix the ingredients well after every addition. Beat in the vanilla. Add the chocolate mixture & continue to mix until combined thoroughly.

4. Combine the flour with baking soda & salt in a small-sized mixing bowl. Give the ingredients a good stir using a whisk. Add half of the prepared flour mixture into the chocolate mixture; followed by the buttermilk; continue to mix the ingredients until incorporated well. Add the leftover flour mixture & mix until the batter is combined well.

5. Spread the prepared batter into the bottom of your pan; don't forget to smooth the edges using a large spatula. Bake in the preheated oven until a toothpick comes out clean, for 25 to 30 minutes. Let cool to room temperature on a wire rack in the pan.

For the Mousse:

1. Sprinkle the gelatin on top of the water in a small bowl; let stand for a couple of minutes. Place the sugar and chocolate in a medium-sized mixing bowl. Next, over medium-high heat in a small saucepan; bring ½ cup of the cream to a simmer.

2. Remove from the heat & add the softened gelatin; give the ingredients a good stir until the gelatin is completely dissolved. Pour the cream on top of the chocolate; whisk until the mixture is smooth and chocolate is melted. Let cool to room temperature until the mixture is slightly thickened, stirring every now and then.

3. Next, whip the leftover cream in the bowl of a stand mixer attached with the whisk attachment for half a minute, until it starts to thicken, at medium speed. Increase the speed to high & continue to whip for half a minute more, until soft peaks form.

4. Use a whisk to mix in ⅓ of the whipped cream into the chocolate mixture. Gently fold the leftover whipped cream into the chocolate mixture using a rubber spatula until no streaks appear.

5. Spoon the prepared chocolate mousse into the pan on top of the chocolate cake. Smooth the top using an offset spatula. Place the cake into the refrigerator again & let chill for 2 hours, until set.

For Ganache:

1. Over medium-high heat in a medium saucepan; heat the butter with cream until the butter is completely melted. Immediately remove the pan from heat; ensure that you don't bring the mixture to a boil.

2. Place the chocolate in a medium heatproof bowl & pour the hot cream on top of the chocolate. Give the ingredients a good stir until the chocolate is completely melted & smooth. Let cool to room temperature.

3. Spread the prepared ganache on top of mousse layer & refrigerate for 40 to 45 minutes, until set.

4. Run a knife along the outer edge of your cake & gently remove it from the pan. Serve with fresh berries

or whipped cream.

CHOCOLATE RASPBERRY GENOISE

Prep Time: 35 minutes

Cooking Time: 50 minutes

Servings: 6 persons

INGREDIENTS

For Genoise cake:

- 7 ounces high-ratio cake shortening
- ¾ pound sugar
- 5 ounces milk
- ¾ pound sifted cake flour
- 2 tablespoons baking powder
- 1 ½ cups whole milk
- 2 teaspoons vanilla extract
- ½ teaspoon salt
- 6 organic eggs, large
- Shortening for greasing pan

For Chocolate chevre mousse:

- 4 ounces chevre cheese
- 2 ounces semisweet chocolate

For Raspberry sauce:

- 3 tablespoons sugar
- 1-pint raspberries
- 3 ounces water
- Juice of ½ lemon, fresh
- ½ teaspoon cream of tartar

For Garnish:

- A pint of raspberries

DIRECTIONS

For Genoise Cake:

1. Preheat your oven to 375 F.
2. Combine the flour with baking powder, sugar, and salt using an electric mixing bowl with the whip attachment, on low speed; scrapping the mixture down from the sides of your bowl using a rubber spatula. Add the half of the milk and eggs. Once eggs and milk are incorporated well; scrape down the

bottom of your bowl completely. Continue to mix the ingredients until no lumps remain, for a couple of minutes.

3. Add the shortening & whip for 1 ½ minutes, on high speed. Add the leftover vanilla extract and milk. Continue to mix until the batter is smooth & incorporated well, on low speed.

4. Grease an 18x13" baking tray with the shortening. Place a piece of parchment paper over the sheet pan and then, lightly coat the parchment paper using the shortening.

5. Pour and evenly spread the prepared cake batter over the sheet pan. Bake in the preheated oven until lightly golden in color, for 25 to 30 minutes; ensure that you don't let it turn brown. Once done; set aside and let cool then, cut the cake into 3" round circles using a cookie or biscuit cutter.

For the Chocolate Chevre Mousse:

1. Heat the chocolate in a double boiler until completely melted. Once done, immediately remove it from the heat. Place the chevre in a medium-sized mixing bowl and then, add the melted chocolate. Whisk the chevre with melted chocolate until completely smooth.

For the Raspberry Sauce:

1. Over medium heat in a medium-sized saucepan; combine the raspberries with cream of tartar, sugar, lemon juice, and water; give the ingredients a good stir and ensure that the sauce don't stick to the bottom of your pan. Continue to cook the sauce and bring it to a slight boil. The remove the saucepan from heat & transfer the mixture to a blender. Blend on high power until the sauce is completely smooth. Get rid of any seeds by passing the sauce through a cheesecloth or strainer.

To Serve:

1. Place a cake round in the middle of your plate. Spread a layer of the prepared chocolate chevre mousse on top of the cake. Place an even layer of whole raspberries over the mousse. Repeat the layers with the cake, raspberries, and mousse. Drizzle the sauce on top of the cake tiers & around the plate. Serve immediately & enjoy.

TRADITIONAL VICTORIA CAKE

Prep Time: 20 minutes

Cooking Time: 25 minutes

Servings: 6 persons

INGREDIENTS

- 1 cup superfine/caster sugar
- 1 cup unsalted butter, softened at room temperature
- 4 medium-sized eggs
- 1 teaspoon baking powder or baking soda
- 1 cup self-rise flour
- ¼ cup milk, whole fat

For Filling:

- Butter-cream & raspberry jam

DIRECTIONS

1. Prepare 2 round baking tins, 6" by lightly greasing & flouring them and then, preheat your oven to 350 F.
2. Cream the butter with sugar until light & fluffy; ensure that the butter is mixed well with the sugar.
3. Crack four eggs into a separate bowl. Work in batches and add the eggs to the batter; mix well on slow speed.
4. Sift the baking powder and flour; add the mixture to the batter.
5. Continue to mix the ingredients until the flour is incorporated well & then add the milk; give the ingredients a good stir until combined well.
6. Evenly divide the prepared cake batter between the prepared cake pans & bake them in the preheated oven until a skewer comes out clean, for 20 to 25 minutes.
7. Once done; remove them from the oven; leaving the cakes in the tins for a couple of minutes then, transfer the cakes to a wire rack to completely cool.
8. Once done, spread the buttercream over one half. Spread the raspberry jam over the other half of the cake & then carefully sandwich the two layers together. Lightly dust the top with powdered sugar (icing); serve immediately & enjoy.

FUDGY PUDGY PUDDING PIE

Prep Time: 20 minutes

Cooking Time: 25 minutes

Servings: 8 persons

INGREDIENTS

- 2 tablespoons cornstarch
- 1 ½ cups milk
- 1 pie crust (9"), baked
- 2 tablespoons all-purpose flour
- 1 ¼ cups white sugar
- 4 large egg yolks
- 1 tablespoon butter
- 2 squares of unsweetened chocolate (1 ounce), chopped
- 1 teaspoon vanilla extract
- ¼ teaspoon salt

DIRECTIONS

1. Combine the sugar with cornstarch, flour & salt in a medium-sized saucepan; whisk until combined

well. Whisk the milk with egg yolks in a separate medium-sized mixing bowl until completely smooth. Slowly stir into the sugar mixture. Cook over medium heat until the mixture comes to a full boil and thickens, stirring constantly. Continue to boil & stir the ingredients for a minute more.

2. Remove from the heat & stir in the chocolate, vanilla, and butter; give the ingredients a good stir until the chocolate and butter is completely melted.

3. Pour into the pie shell. To prevent the skin from forming; don't forget to place a plastic wrap on top of the filling & let chill for a couple of hours. Top with the whipped cream or meringue & some chocolate curls. Enjoy.

CHOCOLATE HAZELNUT MOUSSE TART

Prep Time: 20 minutes

Cooking Time: 4 hours & 20 minutes

Servings: 12 persons

INGREDIENTS

For Crust and Spread:

- 6 ounces thin chocolate wafer cookies
- ½ cup raw, skin-on hazelnuts
- Chocolate Hazelnut Spread
- 6 tablespoons butter, melted

For Mousse and Topping

- 2 large eggs, separated
- 6 ounces bittersweet chocolate, roughly chopped
- 2 tablespoons hazelnut liqueur
- ½ cup whipping cream
- 2 tablespoons sugar
- ½ cup roasted hazelnuts, very roughly chopped

DIRECTIONS

1. Preheat your oven to 350 F.

2. For Crust: Roast the hazelnuts in the preheated oven for 15 to 18 minutes, until turn light golden, on a rimmed baking sheet. Remove the skins by rubbing them in a kitchen towel. Decrease your oven's temperature to 325 F.

3. Whirl the hazelnuts and cookies in a food processor until finely ground. Slowly add the butter & whirl until crumbs begin to clump together; pressing the crumbs on the bottom & up sides of a 9 ½"tart pan with a removable rim.

4. Bake for 7 to 10 more minutes, until the crust is almost set. Let completely cool. Spread the chocolate-hazelnut spread on top of the crust. Let chill for half an hour, until spread is firm.

5. For Mousse: Melt the chocolate with sugar & 2 tablespoon of water over low heat in a small saucepan until completely smooth, for 8 to 10 minutes, stirring every now and then; set aside until ready to use.

6. Beat the eggs whites using a mixer in a medium-sized mixing bowl until stiff peaks hold together. Beat the cream in a separate bowl until stiff. Stir the yolks & liqueur into the prepared chocolate mixture.

7. Gently fold the chocolate mixture into the egg whites and then, fold in the cream until no streaks remain. Pour the mousse into the crust & evenly spread. Sprinkle with the chopped hazelnuts & let chill for several hours, until mousse is firm. Remove the rim from pan & cut into desired wedges.

CHOCOLATE ALMOND FRANGIPANE TART

Prep Time: 20 minutes

Cooking Time: 2 hours & 20 minutes

Servings: 8 persons

INGREDIENTS

- 1 free-range egg, medium, beaten
- 250g plain flour, plus additional for dusting
- 1 tablespoon golden caster sugar
- 150g unsalted butter fridge cold, cut into very small pieces

For Filling:

- 175g softened unsalted butter, at room temperature
- 3 firm conference pears
- 150g plain chocolate
- 2 tablespoons lemon juice, fresh
- ½ teaspoon salt flakes
- 125g ground almonds
- ½ teaspoon baking powder
- 175g golden caster sugar
- 2 free-range eggs, medium, beaten
- ¼ teaspoon vanilla extract
- 75g plain flour
- 15g flaked almonds

DIRECTIONS

1. For Pastry: Put the flour with sugar and butter in a food processor; blend on high power until the mixture

reflects fine breadcrumbs like consistency. With the motor still running, add the egg slowly into the flour mixture. As soon as the dough forms a ball; immediately turn off the motor of your food processor.

2. Roll the pastry out on a well-floured surface, lifting & turning after every couple of rolls. Line a deep fluted 25cm flan tin with the pastry. Place on a sturdy baking tray & lightly prick the base with a large fork. Let chill for half an hour. In the meantime; preheat your oven to 405 F.

3. Line the pastry case with crumpled baking parchment & fill with the baking beans. Bake blind for 20 to 22 minutes and then, remove the beans and paper; continue to cook until the base is very dry, for a couple of more minutes. Remove from the oven & put to one side while you prepare the filling. Decrease your oven's temperature to 320 F.

4. Peel the pears & then, cut them into quarters; get rid of the cores & put the pear quarters into a large-sized mixing bowl. Add the freshly squeezed lemon juice; toss well. Put the chocolate on a clean, large board & chop it roughly.

5. Blend the butter with sugar in a food processor until pale & soft, on high-power. Add the flour followed by ground almonds, vanilla, eggs, baking powder and salt; continue to blend until mixed well. Remove the blade & stir in the chocolate pieces using a large spatula.

6. Evenly spread the almond mixture on top of the cooled pastry case, beginning at the edges and then, head to the middle. Drain the pear quarters & arrange on their sides in a circle around the tart, gently pressing them into the almond mix, narrow ends towards the middle.

7. Bake for half an hour, in the middle rack. Sprinkle the flaked almonds over & bake again until the pears are tender & the frangipane filling turns golden brown and is well risen, for 35 to 40 more minutes; keep an eye on it; don't let it turn too brown. Let stand for 12 to 15 minutes and then carefully lift them from the tin. Serve warm with plenty of crème fraiche and enjoy.

MAPLE BACON CHOCOLATE CHIP COOKIES

Prep Time: 20 minutes

Cooking Time: 20 minutes

Servings: 24 persons

INGREDIENTS

- 1 teaspoon baking powder
- 2 cups all-purpose flour
- 1 teaspoon baking soda
- ¾ cup brown sugar, packed
- 1 cup butter, at room temperature
- ¾ cup white sugar

- 1 teaspoon vanilla extract
- 2 organic eggs, large
- 1 cup bittersweet chocolate chips
- ⅓ cup cooked bacon, chopped
- 1 teaspoon maple extract
- ½ teaspoon salt

DIRECTIONS

1. Line two large-sized baking sheets with the parchment paper and then, preheat your oven to 350 F. Whisk the flour with baking soda, baking powder & salt; set aside.
2. Beat the butter with white sugar, and brown sugar using an electric mixer until completely smooth. Slowly add the egg; continue to beat until blended well into the butter mixture.
3. Add the leftover egg followed by maple extract and vanilla extract; continue to beat until slightly fluffy & blended well. Slowly stir in the flour mixture, mixing until just combined.
4. Stir in the chocolate chips and bacon. Using rounded tablespoonfuls; scoop the mixture over the prepared cookie sheets.
5. Bake for 10 to 12 minutes, until the edges turn golden brown. Remove them from the oven & let cool on the wire rack.

CRISPY COCONUT MACAROONS

Prep Time: 25 minutes

Cooking Time: 25 minutes

Servings: 26 persons

INGREDIENTS

- ⅞ cup condensed milk, sweetened
- 1 bag sweetened flaked coconut (14 ounces)
- 2 eggs whites, large
- 1 teaspoon vanilla extract
- 4 ounces best quality semi-sweet chocolate, chopped
- ¼ teaspoon salt

DIRECTIONS

1. Set 2 oven racks near the middle of your oven. Line 2 large-sized baking sheets with the parchment paper and then, preheat your oven to 325 F.
2. Combine the coconut with vanilla extract and sweetened condensed milk in a medium bowl; mix well & set the mixture aside until ready to use.
3. Beat the egg whites & salt in the bowl of an electric mixer for a minute or two until stiff peaks form. Fold the egg whites into the coconut mixture using a large rubber spatula.

4. Form heaping tablespoons of the prepared mixture into mounds on the baking sheets using two spoons or mini ice cream scoop, spacing approximately an inch apart. Bake in the preheated oven until the tops & edges turn golden, for 22 to 25 minutes, rotating the pans from front to back & top to bottom. Let cool for a couple of minutes on the pans and then, carefully transfer to a wire rack to completely cool.

5. Next, heat the chocolate in a microwave-safe bowl until melted, smooth & creamy; at medium power; stopping & stirring after 30 seconds intervals. Dip the bottoms of the macaroons into the chocolate, letting any excess to drip into the bowl & place them to the lined baking sheets. Place the macaroons in a refrigerator until the chocolate is set, for 10 minutes. Store the cookies at room temperature in an airtight container for a week.

HAZELNUT & CARDAMOM COOKIES

Prep Time: 25 minutes

Cooking Time: 25 minutes

Servings: 20 persons

INGREDIENTS

- ½ cup hazelnuts
- 1 cup all-purpose flour
- ¼ cup sugar
- ⅔ cups butter, at room temperature
- ½ teaspoon each of baking powder & cardamom seeds

DIRECTIONS

1. Preheat your oven to 350 F.
2. Grind the hazelnuts in a blender or food processor.
3. Grind the cardamom seeds using mortar & pestle or food processor.
4. Combine the butter with sugar in a medium-sized mixing bowl. Mix with a wooden spoon or spatula, until combined well. Add flour followed by the ground hazelnut, baking powder & ground cardamom; continue to mix until combined well.
5. Next, mix with your hands until you get dough like consistency.
6. Place the dough between two baking sheets & flatten the dough using a rolling pin; rotating the baking sheets to make it easier to roll the entire dough into the desired size.
7. Once the dough is approximately 32 cm x 25 in size, peel off the top baking sheet from the dough.
8. Cut the cookies using a medium-sized cookie cutter into desired size.
9. Place the cookies on a baking sheet lined baking tray.
10. Bake until the cookies turn dark on the top, for 12 to 15 minutes.
11. Remove the cookies from the oven & set aside to completely cool.
12. Serve; sprinkled with some more of ground cardamom. Enjoy.

ALMOND COFFEE CRISPS

Prep Time: 20 minutes

Cooking Time: 25 minutes

Servings: 6 dozen

INGREDIENTS

- 1 cup shortening
- 2 cups packed brown sugar
- 2 large eggs, room temperature
- ½ cup brewed coffee, room temperature
- 3-½ cups all-purpose flour
- 1 teaspoon baking soda
- 1 teaspoon salt
- 1-½ teaspoons ground cinnamon, divided
- 1 cup chopped almonds, toasted
- 3 tablespoons sugar

DIRECTIONS

1. Cream the shortening with brown sugar in a large-sized mixing bowl until light & fluffy. Slowly add the eggs; beating well after each addition and then, beat in the coffee. Next, combine flour with baking soda, 1 teaspoon of cinnamon and salt; slowly add to the creamed mixture; mix well and then, stir in the almonds.

2. Using rounded teaspoonfuls; drop the prepared batter onto the ungreased baking sheets, approximately 2" apart. Combine the leftover cinnamon with sugar; sprinkle on top of the cookies. Flatten them slightly & bake until firm, for 10 to 12 minutes, at 375 F. carefully remove them to wire racks to completely cool.

CLASSIC ENGLISH CRUMPETS

Prep Time: 25 minutes

Cooking Time: 25 minutes

Servings: 12 persons

INGREDIENTS

- 2 cups plus 2 tablespoons all-purpose flour
- 1 ¼ cups warm water
- 1 teaspoon white sugar
- 2 teaspoons quick-rise instant yeast

- 1 ¼ cups warm milk
- ½ teaspoon salt
- cooking spray

DIRECTIONS

1. Whisk the flour with sugar, yeast & salt in a large-sized mixing bowl.
2. Next, combine milk and water in a separate bowl; quickly whisk the milk mixture into the dry ingredients for a minute or two, until the batter is thick & smooth.
3. Using a kitchen towel; cover & let rise in a warm place for an hour, until turn spongy. Stir the dough to reduce the sponginess.
4. Place a rack into the oven & preheat it to 150 F.
5. Lightly coat a large skillet, crumpet molds or round metal open-top cookie cutters with the cooking spray.
6. Next, over medium to low heat in the skillet; heat up the molds of the metal cutters or molds. Spoon the prepared batter into the molds, filling them approximately halfway full.
7. Let the crumpets to cook for 5 to 6 minutes, until the tops appear nearly dry, the bottoms are browned & popped bubbles appear on top.
8. Lift the molds carefully from the pan using a pair of tongs; remove the molds from crumpets.
9. Flip & place the crumpets back to the skillet; cook the other side for a couple of more minutes, until turn browned.
10. Repeat with the leftover dough. Keep cooked crumpets warm on rack in the preheated oven. Serve and enjoy.

CHOCOLATE BABKA

Prep Time: 20 minutes

Cooking Time: 2 hours & 30 minutes

Servings: 8 persons

INGREDIENTS

For the Bread

- 100g caster sugar
- 2 sachets dried yeast (14g)
- 150g unsalted butter, softened
- 3 eggs, free-range
- 530g plain flour
- zest of 1 orange
- 120ml water
- sunflower oil for greasing

- ⅓ teaspoon salt

For the Chocolate Filling

- 100g pecans, roughly chopped
- 50g icing sugar
- 2 tablespoons caster sugar
- 130g dark chocolate
- 30g cocoa powder
- 120g melted butter

For the Sugar Glaze

- 260g caster sugar
- 160ml water

DIRECTIONS

1. Combine flour with yeast, sugar & zest in a large-sized mixing bowl using your hands. Add the eggs & water; continue to mix until the dough comes together, for a couple of more minutes. Add salt & the butter (a cube at a time); let the butter to completely melt into the dough. Continue to mix the ingredients until elastic, smooth & sticky dough like consistency is achieved, for a couple of more minutes.

2. Lightly coat a large bowl with some sunflower oil; place the dough ball into it. Using a cling film; cover the bowl & let rise for overnight.

3. The next day, prepare the chocolate filling. Combine cocoa powder with icing sugar, melted butter and melted dark chocolate. Continue to beat until smooth, spreadable paste like consistency is achieved.

4. Grease 2 loaf tins, 2 pounds each & line the bottom with the parchment baking paper.

5. Evenly divide the formed dough into parts; work with first part on a floured surface; leaving the leftover dough in the fridge, covered.

6. Roll the dough out onto the surface using a rolling pin and then, trim the edges using a knife to obtain a 38x28cm rectangle. Spread half of the prepared chocolate filling on top of the dough; leaving approximately 2 cm border all around. Sprinkle one tablespoon of caster sugar and half of the pecans.

7. Brush a small amount of water over the long edge of the dough on your left. Roll up the rectangle like a roulade using both hands, beginning from the long side on your right, rolling towards the left side. Completely roll the dough into a perfect, thick log, sitting on its seam.

8. Trim off 2 cm of both ends using a sharp kitchen knife. Gently, cut the roll into two, lengthways, from the top to the bottom. Position the cut sides facing up, gently press the ends together.

9. Lift the right half over the left half. Repeat with the left half over the right half and press the ends together to seal it. Carefully lift the loaf and place into the tin.

10. Repeat the process with the leftover dough. Using a wet tea towel; cover the loaves & leave in a warm place for 1 ½ hours to rise.

11. Preheat your oven to 340 F. Once the cakes have risen, get rid of the tea towels & place them on the

center shelf for half an hour.

12. While the cakes are in the oven; prepare the syrup. Place the sugar & water over a medium heat in a large saucepan. As soon as the syrup starts to boil, and the sugar is dissolved; remove the pan from heat & set aside to cool down.

13. When the cakes are baked; remove them from the oven & brush them with the prepared syrup.

14. Remove the cooked cakes from the tins & let completely cool down. Serve and enjoy.

RUGALACH

Prep Time: 1 hour & 20 minutes

Cooking Time: 20 minutes

Servings: 4 dozen

INGREDIENTS

- ¼ cup granulated sugar plus 9 tablespoons
- 8 ounces cream cheese, at room temperature
- ¼ cup light brown sugar, packed
- 1 teaspoon pure vanilla extract
- ½ cup apricot preserves, pureed in a food processor
- 2 cups all-purpose flour
- ½ pound unsalted butter, at room temperature
- 1 ½ teaspoons ground cinnamon
- 1 cup walnuts, finely chopped
- ¾ cup raisins
- 1 egg beaten with 1 tablespoon milk, for egg wash
- ¼ teaspoon kosher salt

DIRECTIONS

1. Cream the cheese with butter in the bowl of an electric mixer fitted with the paddle attachment until light. Add ¼ cup of granulated sugar followed by vanilla & salt. With the mixer still running on low speed, add the flour & mix until just combined. Dump the prepared dough out onto a well-floured board & roll it out into a large ball. Cut the ball into quarters. Using a plastic wrap; cover each piece & refrigerate for an hour.

2. For Filling: Combine 6 tablespoons of the granulated sugar with ½ teaspoon cinnamon, brown sugar, walnuts, and raisins.

3. Roll each dough ball into a 9" circle on a well-floured board. Evenly spread the dough with 2 tablespoons of the apricot preserves & sprinkle with ½ cup of the filling; lightly pressing the filling into the dough. Cut the circle into 12 equal wedges; cutting the whole circle in quarters and then each quarter into thirds. Starting with the wide edge, roll up each wedge. Place the cookies, points tucked under, on a

parchment paper lined baking sheet. Let chill for half an hour.

4. Preheat your oven to 350 F.

5. Brush each cookie with the egg wash. Combine 3 tablespoons of the granulated sugar with 1 teaspoon of cinnamon & sprinkle the cookies with the prepared mixture. Bake until turn lightly browned, for 15 to 20 minutes. Remove to a wire rack & let completely cool.

BUTTERSCOTCH BROWNIES

Prep Time: 20 minutes

Cooking Time: 30 minutes

Servings: 24 persons

INGREDIENTS

- 1 ½ cups all-purpose flour
- ¾ cup butter
- 3 organic eggs, large
- 1 ½ teaspoon baking powder
- 3 cup brown sugar
- 1 ½ teaspoon vanilla extract
- 1 teaspoon salt

DIRECTIONS

1. Either line a 9x13" brownie pan with parchment paper or coat it lightly with non-stick spray and then, preheat your oven to 350 F.

2. Add softened butter followed by eggs, vanilla and sugar to a large-sized mixing bowl; mix until combined well.

3. Stir the flour with baking powder & salt in a small-sized mixing bowl. Slowly add the flour mixture into the sugar mixture; continue to mix until combined well.

4. Bake in the preheated oven for half an hour & then, carefully remove the brownies from the oven. Let slightly cool before serving.

DATE NUT BREAD

Prep Time: 20 minutes

Cooking Time: 1 hour & 20 minutes

Servings: 3 dozen slices

INGREDIENTS

- 8 ounces dried, pitted dates
- 2 tablespoons butter

- 2 eggs
- 2 cups sugar
- 4 cups flour
- 2 tablespoons baking soda
- 1 teaspoon salt
- 2 teaspoons vanilla
- 1 cup chopped walnuts

DIRECTIONS

1. Preheat your over to 350 F.
2. Remove the tops from 6 to 7 empty soup cans and then, grease them lightly with the butter or oil.
3. Combine the dates with sugar & butter in a medium-sized mixing bowl. Add 2 cups of boiling water & let cool.
4. When done, slowly add the egg; beat well after each addition.
5. Sift the flour with baking soda & salt. Mix with the wet ingredients.
6. Add vanilla & then, mix in the nuts.
7. Fill each soup can approximately ½ full of the prepared batter.
8. Place the cans on to a large-sized baking sheet & bake in the preheated oven for an hour. Let cool & remove the bread from cans. Cut into ½ to 1" slices to serve. Spread the slices with cream cheese.

CHOCOLATE CHIP BISCOTTI

Prep Time: 20 minutes

Cooking Time: 55 minutes

Servings: 36 persons

INGREDIENTS

- 2 organic eggs, large
- ½ cup softened butter
- 2 teaspoons baking powder
- 1 cup brown sugar
- 2 ½ cups all-purpose flour
- 1 teaspoons vanilla extract
- 12 ounces mini chocolate chips
- ½ teaspoon salt

DIRECTIONS

1. Preheat your oven to 350 F.
2. Add brown sugar with butter to a mixer bowl; Beat for a minute, at medium speed.
3. Add vanilla and eggs; continue to mix for a minute more, until combined well.

4. Add flour followed by baking powder & salt; continue to mix until combined well.

5. Fold in the mini chocolate chips.

6. Shape into 2 10x2" logs & place on a greased or lined baking sheet.

7. Bake in the preheated oven for 22 to 25 minutes and then, carefully remove them from the oven; let cool for half an hour.

8. Decrease your oven's temperature to 300 F.

9. Slice the logs into approximately ½" slices & arrange them on the cookie sheet. Bake for 12 to 15 more minutes. Carefully flip the slices over & bake for 15 more minutes.

10. Remove to a wire rack to completely cool & store them in an airtight container.

ALSATIAN GINGERBREAD

Prep Time: 20 minutes

Cooking Time: 50 minutes

Servings: 10 persons

INGREDIENTS

- ½ cup whole wheat flour
- 2 tablespoons brown sugar
- ¼ teaspoon ground allspice
- ½ teaspoon each of ground ginger & ground nutmeg
- 1 ¼ teaspoon baking powder
- ½ cup honey
- 1 organic egg, large
- ¼ teaspoon ground cinnamon
- 4 tablespoons whole milk
- ½ cup rye flour
- ¼ teaspoon ground anise
- 2 teaspoons lemon peel or candied orange, finely diced
- ⅛ teaspoon white pepper
- ¼ teaspoon kosher salt

For Glaze:

- ¼ teaspoon rum
- 1 tablespoon eggnog or milk
- ¼ cup icing sugar

DIRECTIONS

1. Preheat your oven to 350 F.

2. Combine the brown sugar and honey over moderate heat in a small saucepan; gently heat until the

mixture is warm, and sugar is dissolved, stirring frequently.

3. Sift the flours with spices, baking powder, and salt into the bowl of a stand mixer.

4. Whisk the egg with milk in a small-sized mixing bowl.

5. Slowly pour the egg-milk mixture into the flour mixture using the paddle attachment on low speed; stopping & scrapping up the flour as required.

6. Add the brown sugar and warm honey then the diced citrus peel; continue to mix until combined well, on medium speed.

7. Lightly coat with the veggie spray and then line a medium-sized loaf pan with the parchment paper; ensure that it's hanging from the sides.

8. Pour & then scrape the mixture into the prepared pan. Tap the pan a few times to release any air bubbles & bake until the loaf is deep brown, for 40 to 50 minutes. Let cool in the pan for 15 minutes on a rack; removing using the parchment paper. For Glaze: Mix the milk with icing sugar & rum. Make it as thick or thin as you desire. When cooled slightly; drizzle on the cake. Enjoy.

BEAR CLAWS

Prep Time: 20 minutes

Cooking Time: 25 minutes

Servings: 8 persons

INGREDIENTS

- 1 ½ teaspoons cinnamon, divided
- 1 cup apple pie filling
- ¼ cup powdered sugar
- 1 can large refrigerated biscuits (17 ounce)
- 2 teaspoons milk
- 1 tablespoon sugar

DIRECTIONS

1. Preheat your oven to 375 F.

2. Combine the apple pie filling with 1 teaspoon of cinnamon in a small-sized mixing bowl; set aside.

3. Roll each biscuit out to a 6" long oval on a floured surface.

4. Spoon the prepared apple mixture into the middle of each & fold the dough on top to bottom; pinching the edges to seal.

5. Cut three 1" long slits toward the middle of each biscuit from the rounded edge at even intervals.

6. Arch the tops of the biscuits enough to just open the slits.

7. Combine the granulated sugar with leftover cinnamon in a small-sized mixing bowl.

8. Evenly sprinkle on top of the biscuits.

9. Place on a baking sheets, lightly greased & bake in the preheated oven until turn golden brown, for 10 to

12 minutes.

10. Combine the milk and powdered sugar; drizzle the mixture on top of the bear claws. Serve warm and enjoy.

HUMMINGBIRD BREAD PUDDING

Prep Time: 25 minutes

Cooking Time: 45 minutes

Servings: 8 persons

INGREDIENTS

- 5 organic eggs, large
- 1 loaf French bread (14-ounce); cut into 1" cubes (approximately 12 cups cut)
- 4 cups whole milk
- 1 teaspoon ground cinnamon
- 2 teaspoons vanilla extract
- 1 cup white sugar
- 2 bananas, diced
- 1 can pineapple tidbits (8-ounce), drained
- ¼ cup melted butter
- 1 cup pecans, chopped
- ½ cup light brown sugar, firmly packed

For Salted Caramel Sauce:

- ½ cup heavy whipping cream
- 1 cup firmly packed light brown sugar
- ½ cup butter
- ½ teaspoon salt

DIRECTIONS

1. Lightly coat a 9x13" baking dish with some nonstick cooking spray; set aside and then, preheat your oven to 350 F.
2. Whisk the eggs with vanilla, white sugar, whole milk, and cinnamon in a medium-sized mixing bowl. Place the cubed bread in a large-sized mixing bowl; pour the prepared egg-milk mixture on top of the bread. Let rest for a couple of minutes, stirring once or twice.
3. Add the drained pineapple tidbits and diced banana to the bread mixture; give the ingredients a good stir until combined well. Pour the prepared mixture into the baking dish. Sprinkle the pecans & brown sugar on top & then, drizzle with the melted butter.
4. Bake in the preheated oven until the middle is just set, for 45 to 50 minutes.
5. For Caramel Sauce: Combine the brown sugar with butter, whipping cream & salt over moderate heat in

a medium-sized saucepan. Continue to cook & bring the mixture to a boil; cook for 2 to 3 minutes.

6. Serve the bread pudding warm with the prepared caramel sauce drizzled on top.

ESPRESSO MERINGUE & WALNUT CAKE

Prep Time: 20 minutes

Cooking Time: 3 hours & 20 minutes

Servings: 8 persons

INGREDIENTS

- 1 ½ cups heavy cream
- ⅔ cup brown sugar
- 10 ½ tablespoons softened butter, at room temperature
- 1 teaspoon baking powder
- 4 teaspoons espresso powder
- ½ vanilla bean
- 1 tablespoon maple syrup
- 1 ⅓ cups flour
- 5 large egg yolks
- ⅓ cup milk
- 5 large egg whites
- 1 cup granulated sugar
- ½ cup walnuts, chopped & toasted
- 2 teaspoons cinnamon
- 1 teaspoon salt

DIRECTIONS

1. Separate the eggs; cover the whites with a clean cloth and let sit on the counter for overnight. Pour the cream into a large-sized saucepan. Split & scrape the vanilla bean into the cream; heat until just starts boiling. Once done; immediately remove it from the heat & let cool. Cover & let chill for overnight.

2. The following day: Prepare a 9x12" cake pan with the buttered parchment and then, preheat your oven to 350 F.

3. Next, cream the butter with brown sugar in the bowl of a stand mixer attached with a paddle attachment for a couple of minutes, until fluffy & creamy.

4. Whisk the flour with espresso powder, baking powder & salt. Add the prepared mixture to butter-sugar in 3 increments; don't forget to mix the ingredients well after each addition.

5. Whisk the egg yolks with milk and then, add to the batter in 3 increments, incorporating well after each addition. Scrape the prepared batter into the pan.

6. Next, whip the egg whites in a clean mixing bowl until foamy, for a couple of minutes. Add cinnamon and sugar; continue to whip until soft peaks form.

7. Spread the meringue on top of the cake batter; cover with the toasted walnuts & bake in the preheated oven until the meringue is crackly, for 35 to 40 minutes. Let the cake to completely cool.

8. In the meantime, remove the vanilla bean from cream. Add in the maple syrup & whip the cream until soft peaks form. Cut the cake in half & place one half, meringue side up on a cake plate. Cover with the whipped cream. Top with the leftover half, meringue side up. Let sit for a couple of hours. Serve with a dark chocolate sauce punched up with a few dashes of walnut bitters.

CRANBERRY GINGER UPSIDE-DOWN CAKE

Prep Time: 20 minutes

Cooking Time: 1 hour & 50 minutes

Servings: 10 persons

INGREDIENTS

- 3 cups cranberries, fresh
- 1 ½ cups all-purpose flour
- ¾ cup packed light brown sugar
- 2 tablespoons butter
- 1 ½ tablespoons fresh ginger, peeled & grated
- 2 teaspoons baking powder
- ⅔ cup fat-free whipped topping, frozen & thawed
- 1 cup granulated sugar
- ¼ cup softened butter, at room temperature
- 2 egg yolks, large
- ½ cup milk, fat-free
- 1 teaspoon vanilla extract
- ¼ teaspoon cream of tartar
- 2 egg whites, large
- ¼ teaspoon salt

DIRECTIONS

1. Preheat your oven to 350 F.

2. Lightly coat a 9" round cake pan with some cooking spray and heat it over moderate heat. Once hot; add 2 tablespoons of butter & brown sugar to the pan and cook until the butter is completely melted, stirring frequently. Stir in the ginger & cook for a minute more, stirring frequently. Remove from the heat; arrange the cranberries over the brown sugar mixture.

3. Lightly spoon the flour into dry measuring cups; leveling it well using a sharp knife. Combine flour with baking powder & salt. Combine ¼ cup of butter with granulated sugar in a large-sized mixing bowl; beat with a mixer until completely fluffy, at high speed. Slowly add the egg yolks, beat well after each addition and then, add flour mixture & milk alternately to the butter mixture, starting and ending the process with the flour mixture; mix well after each addition. Beat in the vanilla.

4. Beat the cream of tartar with egg whites using a mixer until stiff peaks form, at medium speed. Fold the egg whites into the prepared batter; pour the batter on top of the cranberries. Bake until a wooden pick comes out clean, for 50 to 55 minutes, at 350 F. Let cool in the pan for 12 to 15 minutes; run a knife around the outside edge & place a plate upside down on top of the cake pan; carefully invert the prepared cake over the plate. Top each serving with some whipped topping & enjoy.

NUTELLA CREPE CAKE

Prep Time: 1 hour & 30 minutes

Cooking Time: 50 minutes

Servings: 14 persons

INGREDIENTS

For Crepe Cake Cream:

- 14 ounces condensed milk
- 1 ½ cup softened unsalted butter, at room temperature
- 3 tablespoons cocoa powder
- ½ cup Nutella

For Crepes:

- 2 cup milk
- ½ cup sugar
- 3 tablespoons cocoa powder
- 1 cup all-purpose flour
- 6 organic eggs
- ½ cup oil

DIRECTIONS

1. Prepare the crepes per the instructions mentioned on the crepe recipe (roughly 15 crepes).

2. Combine the butter with condensed milk, Nutella and cocoa powder in a stand-up mixer. Whisk the ingredients well until completely smooth

3. Apply an equal quantity of the cream between each layer of crepe.

4. Apply the leftover cream on the outside; covering the edges as well.

5. Decorate the crepes with some chocolate and hazelnuts. Let rest for overnight before serving.

CHAI SPICE CAKE WITH ORANGE CARDAMOM FROSTING

Prep Time: 20 minutes

Cooking Time: 30 minutes

Servings: 16 persons

INGREDIENTS

For the Cake:

- 1 ½ cups whole wheat flour
- 1 teaspoon baking soda
- 2 ½ teaspoons chai spice
- 1 cup cane sugar
- ¼ cup extra-virgin olive oil
- 1 cup unsweetened almond milk
- ½ teaspoon kosher salt
- 1 teaspoon vanilla extract

For the Frosting:

- 2 cans coconut milk (400 ml each), full fat (refrigerated for a day)
- 1 teaspoon orange zest
- 2 teaspoons maple syrup
- 1 tablespoon orange juice, freshly squeezed
- ½ teaspoon ground cardamom

Other Topping, Optional:

- ¼ cup shredded coconut, unsweetened, toasted

DIRECTIONS

1. Lightly grease a 9" square pan with butter and then, preheat your oven to 350 F.

2. Whisk the flour with baking soda, spice, sugar & salt in a large-sized mixing bowl. Add the milk, vanilla and oil; stir or whisk until combined well.

3. Pour the prepared batter into the pan & bake in the preheated oven until a tooth pick comes out clean, for 25 to 30 minutes. Remove from the oven & let completely cool on the wire rack.

4. Scoop the solidified coconut milk out in a deep mixing bowl (reserve or discard the coconut water). Beat the coconut milk using an electric mixer for a minute, on high power; scrapping down the sides & add

the maple syrup, cardamom, orange juice and orange zest. Continue to mix until the frosting is light & fluffy, for a couple of more minutes, on high.

5. Evenly spread the prepared frosting over the cooled cake & top with the toasted coconut. Cut into 16 squares; serve and enjoy.

CARAMELIZED FIG CAKE WITH LEMON ANGLAISE

Prep Time: 5 minutes

Cooking Time: 55 minutes

Servings: 8 persons

INGREDIENTS

For Fig Cake:

- 1 ½ teaspoons vanilla
- 3 cups figs, thinly sliced
- 1 ½ teaspoons sugar
- 3 tablespoons avocado oil
- 1 ¼ cup flour
- ¼ cup almonds, sliced
- 1 ½ teaspoons baking powder
- ¼ teaspoon baking soda
- 1 organic egg, large
- ½ cup coconut milk
- 1 ½ tablespoons dry red wine
- 5 tablespoons honey
- 1 ½ tablespoons lemon juice, freshly squeezed
- Zest of 1 lemon, fresh
- ¼ teaspoon salt

For Lemon Anglaise:

- 1 cup coconut milk
- 2 teaspoons lemon juice, fresh-squeezed
- ¼ cup honey
- 1 cup soy milk
- ¼ teaspoon lemon extract
- Zest of 1 lemon, fresh
- ¼ teaspoon vanilla extract

- 1 teaspoon turmeric
- 1 ½ teaspoons cornstarch or arrowroot
- A pinch of salt

DIRECTIONS

For Fig Cake:

1. Preheat your oven to 350 F.
2. Grease a 9" cake pan with butter and then, line it with the parchment paper, grease it again.
3. Sprinkle the pan with sugar and then, line with the thinly sliced figs.
4. Grind the almonds in a food processor.
5. Combine the almonds with egg, flour, baking soda, baking powder & salt in a large-sized mixing bowl; mix well.
6. Combine the milk with vanilla, avocado oil, red wine, honey, lemon juice, and zest in a separate bowl; whisk well.
7. Pour the wet ingredients into dry ingredients & gently fold them together until combined well.
8. Pour this mixture over the figs.
9. Bake in the preheated oven until a toothpick comes out clean, for 35 to 40 minutes.
10. Remove & let cool for a couple of minutes and then, remove from the pan; ensure that you remove the parchment paper as well.

For Lemon Anglaise:

1. Combine the entire ingredients of lemon anglaise in a saucepan and whisk well.
2. Heat it over medium heat until it starts simmering, stirring consistently.
3. Cook until thickened, for 5 to 7 minutes; remove from the heat.
4. Let cool for a couple of minutes and then strain the lemon zest out; place the lemon anglaise in a refrigerator.
5. Serve the cake warm with cooled lemon anglaise spooned on top of each piece. Enjoy.

DARK BUTTERCREAM CUPCAKES

Prep Time: 20 minutes

Cooking Time: 35 minutes

Servings: 12 persons

INGREDIENTS

- ¼ cup plus 2 tablespoons unsweetened cocoa powder
- 1 large egg
- ½ teaspoon baking soda
- 1 teaspoon vanilla extract
- ¼ cup unsalted butter, melted

- 3 tablespoons vegetable oil
- 1 large egg yolk
- ¾ cup plus 2 tablespoons all-purpose flour
- 1 cup granulated sugar
- ¼ cup heavy cream
- A heaping ¼ teaspoon of salt
- ½ cup boiling water

For Chocolate Butter cream:

- 6 tablespoons unsweetened cocoa powder
- ¾ cup softened butter, at room temperature
- 2 ½ cups sugar, powdered
- 1 teaspoon vanilla extract
- 2 - 3 tablespoons heavy cream

DIRECTIONS

For the Chocolate Cupcakes:

1. Preheat your oven to 350 F.
2. Whisk the cocoa powder with baking soda in a large-sized mixing bowl, heat proof. Carefully pour in the boiling water & continue to whisk until mixture is well blended and bubbling subsides; let cool for a couple of minutes.
3. In the meantime, blend the melted butter with granulated sugar, vegetable oil, vanilla & salt using an electric hand mixer in a separate large-sized mixing bowl for half a minute, until combined well, on low speed.
4. Mix in the egg and then, the eggs yolk. Blend in the lukewarm cocoa mixture and then, blend in the heavy cream. Add flour & continue to blend until combined well; scraping down the sides & bottom of your bowl, as required.
5. Evenly divide the prepared batter among 12 paper lined muffin cups; filling each approximately ⅔ full.
6. Bake for 17 to 20 minutes, until a toothpick comes out clean.
7. Remove from the oven & let cool in the muffin pan for several minutes then, transfer them to the wire rack to completely cool. Frost with the chocolate buttercream frosting. Serve and enjoy.

For the Chocolate Buttercream Frosting:

1. Cream the butter in the bowl of an electric stand mixer attached with the paddle attachment for a minute or two, until completely fluffy.
2. Mix in the cocoa powder, powdered sugar, 2 tablespoons cream & vanilla; continue to mix until light & fluffy. If required, feel free to add more of cream to the mixture to make it thin.

WHITE CHOCOLATE CUPCAKES WITH

RASPBERRY MOUSSE

Prep Time: 2 hours

Cooking Time: 25 minutes

Servings: 12 persons

INGREDIENTS

For Vanilla Cake Layers:

- 2 ½ cups All-purpose flour
- ¼ cup water
- 1 ½ cups sugar
- ¾ cup softened unsalted butter, at room temperature
- 6 large egg whites, at room temperature
- ¾ cup farms milk, at room temperature
- 1 tablespoon vanilla extract
- ¾ cup sour cream
- 4 teaspoons baking powder
- ½ teaspoon salt

For White Chocolate Mousse:

- 1 cup heavy whipping cream, cold, divided
- 6 ounces white chocolate chips
- ½ cup powdered sugar

For Raspberry Mousse and Filling:

- 3 ½ cups raspberries
- 1 ⅔ cups powdered sugar
- 2 ¾ cups heavy whipping cream, cold
- 1 ½ tablespoons sugar
- 3 ½ teaspoons unflavored gelatin, powdered
- 2 teaspoons cornstarch

DIRECTIONS

For Cake Layers:

1. Prepare 3 cake pans, 8" each with the parchment paper circles in the bottom & coat the sides with some butter. Preheat your oven to 350 F.
2. Cream the sugar with butter in a large-sized mixing bowl for 3 to 4 minutes, until light in color & fluffy.
3. Add the vanilla extract and sour cream; mix until combined well.
4. Work in batches & add the egg whites until combined well; mixing well after each addition. Scrape down the sides of your bowl as required and ensure that the entire ingredients are incorporated well.

5. Combine the dry ingredients in a separate bowl and then, combine the water with milk in a small measuring cup.

6. Add half of the dry ingredients into the batter; mix until combined well. Add in the milk mixture & continue to mix until combined well. Add the leftover dry ingredients & mix until combined well; scrapping down the sides of your bowl as required.

7. Evenly divide the batter between the prepared cakes pans & bake until a toothpick comes out with a few crumbs, for 20 to 23 minutes.

8. Remove the cakes from oven & let cool for 2 to 3 minutes and then, remove to cooling racks to completely cool.

For White Chocolate Mousse:

1. Heat ¼ cup of the heavy cream until it just begins to boil and then, pour it on top of the white chocolate chips. Using a clear wrap; cover for 3-4 minutes and then, whisk until completely smooth; set aside for a couple of minutes to cool.

2. Whip the leftover ¾ cup of the heavy whipping cream with powdered sugar in a large-sized mixer bowl attached with a whisk attachment for a minute, until stiff peaks form.

3. Carefully fold approximately ⅓ of the whipped cream into the cooled white chocolate mixture until combined well.

4. Fold in the leftover whipped cream until combined well. Set the mousse in a refrigerator until ready to use.

For Raspberry Mousse and Filling:

1. Puree the raspberries in a food processor and then, strain the mixture using a fine mesh sieve; discarding the seeds.

2. For Raspberry Filling: Add half a cup of the prepared raspberry puree along with the sugar and cornstarch to a small-sized saucepan. Slowly heat the ingredients over medium heat until the mixture starts to boil and thicken. Cook for a minute and then, remove it from the heat; set aside to cool.

3. For Raspberry Mousse: Add the leftover raspberry puree to a large-sized dish.

4. Evenly sprinkle with the powdered gelatin & let stand for a couple of minutes.

5. Heat the gelatin & puree in the microwave until warm & smooth, in 10-second intervals; set aside to cool to room temperature

6. Next, whip the powdered sugar with heavy whipping cream in a large mixer bowl attached with the whisk attachment for a minute or two, until stiff peaks form.

7. Add the cooled raspberry gelatin mixture into the whipped cream & gently whip until combined well. Refrigerate until ready to use.

To Assemble the Cake:

1. Remove the domes from the top of the cakes using a large serrated knife. Place the first cake on a cardboard cake round or a serving plate.

2. Pipe a dam of raspberry mousse around the edge of your cake and then, evenly spread a few tablespoons

of the raspberry filling into the middle.

3. Add half of the prepared white chocolate mousse over the raspberry filling; spreading it into an even layer.
4. Add the second cake layer & one more layer of the raspberry filling & white chocolate mousse.
5. Top the cake with the leftover cake layer.
6. Frost the outside of your cake.
7. Pipe swirls around the top of your cake using ATECO tip 808. Finish off the cake with some more shaved white chocolate & raspberries. Refrigerate until ready to serve.

S'MORES CUPCAKES

Prep Time: 3 hours & 20 minutes

Cooking Time: 20 minutes

Servings: 14 persons

INGREDIENTS

For Chocolate Cupcake:

- 1 ½ cup all-purpose flour
- 1 cup granulated sugar
- ¼ cup cocoa powder, unsweetened
- 1 teaspoon baking soda
- ½ teaspoons baking powder
- 2 teaspoons vanilla extract
- 1 tablespoon white vinegar
- ½ cup canola oil
- 1 cup brewed coffee
- ½ teaspoon fine sea salt

For Milk Chocolate Ganache:

- ¾ cup each of chopped milk chocolate, and heavy cream

For Milk Chocolate Buttercream Frosting:

- 1 ½ cups powdered sugar sifted
- ½ cup unsalted butter room temperature
- 1 teaspoon vanilla extract
- 2 tablespoons cocoa powder
- ¾ cup milk chocolate ganache

For Marshmallow Frosting

- ½ cup granulated sugar

- 2 large egg whites
- ¼ teaspoon cream of tartar
- 1 teaspoon vanilla extract
- ⅛ teaspoon fine sea salt

To Assemble

- 1.7 ounces graham cracker crumbs, crushed

DIRECTIONS

For Chocolate Cupcake:

1. Grease a 12-cupcake pan with butter and flour or line it with cupcake liners and then, preheat your oven to 350 F.
2. Sift the flour with baking soda, sugar, cocoa powder, baking powder & salt in a large-sized mixing bowl.
3. Combine the coffee with vinegar, oil and vanilla in a separate bowl. Pour the dry mixture on top of the wet ingredients. Briefly whisk until incorporated well; ensure that you don't overmix the ingredients. Stop the whisking process as soon as you see no more streaks of the dry mixture.
4. Evenly distribute the prepared batter in the cupcake pan & bake for 15 to 20 minutes.
5. Remove & let cool.

For Milk Chocolate Ganache:

1. Finely chop the milk chocolate & place it in a heat proof bowl.
2. Heat the heavy cream to almost a boil over medium heat. Turn the heat off as soon as you could see bubbles appearing on the surface.
3. Pour the hot cream on top of the chocolate.
4. Let stand for a couple of seconds.
5. Mix with a spatula until the chocolate has melted thoroughly and you end up with a luscious & smooth mixture.
6. Reserve approximately ¾ cup of the prepared ganache for frosting. Let cool down for an hour.
7. Set ¼ cup of the ganache aside for the filling part.
8. Place the portion that you saved for the filling in the fridge.

For Milk Chocolate Buttercream Frosting

1. Place the butter in the bowl of a stand mixer.
2. Cream for a minute on medium to high speed.
3. With the mixer off, immediately add the sifted sugar.
4. Mix until incorporated well, on low speed.
5. Once done; whip for a minute, on high speed this time.
6. Add in the vanilla extract & continue to whip until combined well, for 30 more seconds.
7. Add the ganache & whip for a minute or two more, until combined well.
8. Add a few tablespoons of sifted cocoa powder to the buttercream & whip until combined well.

9. Feel free to add a few teaspoons of milk; if the buttercream appears to be too thick until you get your desired consistency.

10. Similarly, add some more of powdered sugar, if buttercream appears to be too runny. Add the ganache after it has completely cooled down.

For Marshmallow Frosting

1. Mix the entire ingredients (excluding vanilla extract) together in the bowl of your stand mixer.

2. Set the bowl over a pot of simmering water over medium heat.

3. While the mixture sits in the double boiler; don't forget to whisk the ingredients.

4. Move the bowl to the mixer.

5. Whip with the whisk attachment on high speed for 3 to 5 minutes.

6. Add vanilla & continue to mix until combined well.

To Assemble

1. Remove the middle of your cupcakes using a small teaspoon.

2. Fill each cupcake with approximately 2 teaspoons of the reserved Ganache filling.

3. Place the cupcake tops on their places.

4. Frost with the Milk Chocolate Buttercream.

5. Sprinkle a few graham cracker crumbs on the sides of your frosting and then, place it in the refrigerator while you prepare the marshmallow frosting.

6. Top the cupcakes with a bit of the marshmallow frosting.

7. Feel free to toast the marshmallow frosting using a torch, if desired.

BANANA CUPCAKES WITH CINNAMON CREAM CHEESE FROSTING

Prep Time: 20 minutes

Cooking Time: 25 minutes

Servings: 18 persons

INGREDIENTS

- 2 cups all-purpose flour
- ½ cup dark or light brown sugar, packed
- 1 teaspoon ground cinnamon
- ¼ cup plain yogurt or sour cream, at room temperature
- 1 teaspoon baking soda
- ½ cup buttermilk, at room temperature
- 1 ½ cups banana, mashed
- ½ cup softened butter, unsalted, to room temperature

- 2 large eggs, at room temperature
- ½ cup granulated sugar
- 2 teaspoons pure vanilla extract
- ¾ teaspoon salt

For Cinnamon Cream Cheese Frosting:

- 3 cups confectioners' sugar, plus additional ¼ cup if required
- ½ cup softened butter, unsalted, at room temperature
- 8 ounces block cream cheese, full-fat, softened, to room temperature
- ½ teaspoon ground cinnamon
- 1 teaspoon pure vanilla extract
- ⅛ teaspoon salt

Optional:

- Banana chips and/or salted caramel

DIRECTIONS

1. Preheat your oven to 350 F. Line a muffin pan (12 cups) with cupcake liners and then, line a second pan with 6 liners.
2. Make the cupcakes: Whisk the flour, baking soda, cinnamon, and salt together. Set aside.
3. Using a handheld or stand mixer fitted with a paddle or whisk attachment, beat the butter and both sugars together on high speed until smooth and creamy, about 2 minutes. Scrape down the sides and up the bottom of the bowl with a rubber spatula as needed. Add the eggs, yogurt, and vanilla, then beat on medium-high speed until combined. Scrape down the sides and up the bottom of the bowl as needed. Beat in the mashed banana. With the mixer on low speed, add the dry ingredients until just incorporated. With the mixer still running on low, slowly pour in the buttermilk until combined well; ensure that you don't over mix the ingredients and there are no flour pockets at the bottom of your bowl.
4. Spoon or pour the prepared batter into the liners; filling each approximately ⅔ full. Bake in the preheated oven until a toothpick comes out clean, for 18 to 20 minutes. Let the cupcakes to completely cool before you begin the frosting process.
5. For Frosting: Beat the butter with cream cheese using a stand or handheld mixer attached with a whisk or paddle attachment in a large bowl until smooth & creamy, on high speed. Add 3 confectioners' vanilla, sugar, cinnamon & salt. Continue to beat for 30 more seconds, on low speed and then, switch to high speed; beat for a minute or two more.
6. Frost the cooled cupcakes per your likings and top with the optional banana chip and/or salted caramel. Store leftovers in a refrigerator.

FLOURLESS CHOCOLATE ESPRESSO CAKE

Prep Time: 20 minutes

Cooking Time: 45 minutes

Servings: 6 persons

INGREDIENTS

Flourless Espresso Chocolate Cake

- 180 g unsalted butter, plus more for the cake pan
- 250 g 65% -70% cacao dark chocolate
- 70 g strong espresso, freshly brewed
- 20 g cocoa powder, unsweetened
- 260 g almond or hazelnut flour
- 180 g sugar
- 6 free-range eggs
- 5 g sea salt

For Silky Espresso Glaze:

- 100 g strong espresso, freshly brewed
- 15 g cocoa powder, unsweetened
- 80 g sugar

DIRECTIONS

1. Preheat your oven to 375 F. Melt the butter and chocolate in a bowl placed over a saucepan of simmering water. Add the freshly brewed strong espresso & salt to the butter-chocolate mix; give the ingredients a good stir & remove from the heat to cool.
2. Beat the sugar and eggs for a couple of minutes in a bowl set over a saucepan of simmering water, until thick & pale.
3. Pour the chocolate mixture into the egg mixture & continue to beat for 2 to 3 more minutes. Add the unsweetened cacao and hazelnut flour; stir well.
4. For Glaze: Bring the sugar with freshly brewed strong espresso and cacao to a boil over moderate heat in a saucepan. Let simmer for 2 minutes, stirring every now and then. Set aside until ready to use.
5. Lightly coat the cake pan with some butter. Decrease your oven's temperature to 350 F. Pour the prepared batter into the cake pan & bake for 35 to 40 minutes, until set. Serve with vanilla ice cream and/or cacao glaze.

MOCHA DACQUOISE CAKE

Prep Time: 25 minutes

Cooking Time: 4 hours & 30 minutes

Servings: 12 persons

INGREDIENTS

For the Almond Meringue and Buttercream:

- 2 ⅓ cups granulated sugar
- 8 large egg whites
- 12 ounces unsalted butter, softened
- 3 ¼ cups plus 1 tablespoon blanched almond flour
- 1 tablespoon cornstarch
- 7 large egg yolks
- 1 cup sugar
- ⅔ cup coffee

For the Chantilly:

- 2 cups heavy cream
- 1 tablespoons dark rum
- ½ cup confectioners' sugar, plus more for garnishing

For Drizzling:

- Chocolate sauce, Hot fudge, or Bittersweet ganache

DIRECTIONS

1. Preheat your oven to 250 F.
2. For Meringue: Beat the egg whites in a stand mixer for 2 to 3 minutes, until very stiff peaks form, on high speed.
3. In the meantime, pulse the almond flour with sugar & cornstarch in a food processor until you get fine sand like consistency. Transfer the mixture to a large-sized mixing bowl.
4. Trace three 10" circles out on parchment paper. Set them on 1-2 large baking sheets lined with the silicone mats.
5. Working in batches, fold the egg whites into the almond mixture using a rubber spatula until combined thoroughly. Evenly scoop the mixture onto the traced circles and fill the circles by evenly spreading the meringue using an offset spatula.
6. Bake in the preheated oven for 2 hours & 20 minutes, until an even golden brown is achieved, rotating the pans after every 10 minutes.
7. Remove & let slightly cool. Work very slowly & carefully get rid of the parchment.
8. For Buttercream: Add the coffee with sugar over medium heat in a high-sided saucepan. Set a candy thermometer into the pan & heat until the thermometer reflects 265 F.
9. In the meantime, whisk the egg yolks in the clean bowl of a stand mixer for 5 to 8 minutes, until the volume has tripled, and the color has lightened significantly.
10. Once done, remove & slowly pour the mixture into the yolks, continue to whisk on medium to low speed for several minutes, letting the mixture to completely cool. Once done, slowly add the butter & continue to whisk until incorporated well then, add the other addition.
11. Place one meringue round on a cake platter. Evenly spread the buttercream over the meringue using an

offset spatula within ½" of the edge. Carefully place the second shell on top; applying very slight pressure and then chill.

12. For Chantilly: Whisk the confectioners' sugar with heavy cream & rum in the clean bowl of the mixer until stiff peaks form.

13. Evenly spread all of the Chantilly over the meringue within ½ inch of the edge as you did the buttercream using an offset spatula and then place the final meringue on top. Return the dacquoise to the refrigerator for overnight.

14. Just before serving, don't forget to lightly dust the surface of your cake with some confectioners' sugar. Slice with a clean, hot knife and garnish slices with a drizzle of hot fudge. Enjoy.

FLOURLESS FUDGE CAKE

Prep Time: 20 minutes

Cooking Time: 2 hours & 20 minutes

Servings: 6 persons

INGREDIENTS

- ½ cup ground flaxseed
- 1 teaspoon vanilla
- ½ cup cocoa powder
- 1 teaspoon baking soda
- 2 tablespoons nut butter
- 1 organic egg, large
- ½ cup plus 2 tablespoons sweet potato puree
- 6 tablespoons honey
- ¼ cup chocolate chips
- A pinch of salt

DIRECTIONS

1. For easy cleanup; grease a 9×5" loaf pan with some butter and then, line it with the parchment paper. Once done; preheat your oven to 350 F.

2. Stir the flax seed with baking soda, cocoa powder & salt in a large-sized mixing bowl. Whisk the vanilla with egg, honey, nut butter & sweet potato puree in a separate bowl until completely smooth. Add the wet ingredients into the dry; give the ingredients a good stir until combined well. Fold in the chocolate chips.

3. Evenly spoon the batter over the prepared loaf pan; smooth the top using the back of a large spoon.

4. Bake in the preheated oven until the cake is no longer wobbly, for 40 to 50 minutes. Let cool for several minutes and then, remove the cake from the pan; serve and enjoy.

APPLE PECAN TORTE

Prep Time: 20 minutes

Cooking Time: 2 hours & 20 minutes

Servings: 8 persons

INGREDIENTS

- 1 tablespoon nondairy margarine or unsalted butter
- 2 (6 ounces each) sweet red apples, such as Jonagold or Braeburn, peeled, cored & sliced ⅛" thick
- 1 teaspoon ground cinnamon
- ¾ cup granulated sugar
- 1 tablespoon lemon juice, fresh
- 2 tablespoons sweet kosher wine
- 1 ¼ cups pecans, toasted, finely ground
- Vegetable oil cooking spray
- ¼ cup finely ground matzo meal or matzo cake meal
- 6 organic eggs, large, at room temperature, separated
- Confectioners' sugar, for garnish
- ½ teaspoon salt

DIRECTIONS

1. Toss the apples with fresh lemon juice. Next, over medium-high heat in a large skillet; heat the butter until melted. Add apples followed by ½ teaspoon cinnamon & ¼ cup of granulated sugar; give the ingredients a good toss. Continue to cook the mixture for 2 to 3 more minutes, until the apples turn soft. Add wine & cook for a couple of more minutes, until the apples are very syrupy and almost absorb the wine.

2. Coat a 9" springform pan with the cooking spray and then, preheat your oven to 350 F. Whisk the yolks with ¼ cup of granulated sugar using an electric mixer for 2 to 3 minutes, until pale & thick, on medium to high speed. Transfer the mixture to a large bowl; fold in the matzo cake meal, pecans, apples, and leftover cinnamon.

3. Whisk the whites, leftover granulated sugar, and salt in a clean bowl of a mixer for a couple of minutes, until stiff, glossy peaks form. Work in batches; gently fold the whites into the prepared batter. Pour into the pan. Bake in the preheated oven for 30 to 35 minutes, until a toothpick comes out clean and the top turns brown; let cool.

4. Run an offset spatula or a knife around edge of your torte. Remove it from the pan & garnish with the confectioners' sugar.

IRISH CREAM SCONES

Prep Time: 20 minutes

Cooking Time: 20 minutes

Servings: 8 persons

INGREDIENTS

For Scones:

- 1 cup Irish-Style flour or 100% whole wheat flour
- 2 teaspoons baking powder
- 1 cup All-purpose flour, unbleached
- ¼ cup Irish Cream liqueur
- 3 tablespoons sugar
- ¼ cup milk
- 8 tablespoons unsalted butter, cold
- ½ cup butterscotch chips, optional
- 1 large egg
- ½ teaspoon salt

For Glaze:

- ⅓ cup butterscotch chips
- 2 tablespoons Irish Cream liqueur

DIRECTIONS

1. For Scones: Position the rack in the upper third and then, preheat your oven to 425 F. Lightly grease a large-sized baking sheet or line it with the parchment.
2. Combine the flours with sugar, baking powder, and salt; mix well.
3. Work the butter into the flour mixture until crumbly unevenly and you could see a few larger, pea-sized pieces of the butter.
4. At this point of time, toss in the optional butterscotch chips.
5. Mix the egg with milk, and liqueur; mix well and then, add to the butter-flour mixture; give the ingredients a good stir until the dough holds together and is moistened evenly.
6. Drop the prepared dough (approximately ⅓ -cupfuls) onto the baking sheet.
7. Bake in the preheated oven until turn golden, for 15 to 18 minutes.
8. Once done; remove the scones from oven & transfer them to a rack for 5 to 10 minutes to cool down.
9. For Glaze: Combine the butterscotch chips with liqueur in a microwave-safe bowl; microwave for 30 seconds, on high heat; give it a good stir until completely smooth.
10. Drizzle the prepared glaze on top of the warm scones. Serve warm & enjoy.

FLAKY CREAM CHEESE SCONES

Prep Time: 25 minutes

Cooking Time: 20 minutes

Servings: 15 persons

INGREDIENTS

For Scones:

- 3 cups all-purpose flour, unbleached
- ¼ cup cornstarch
- 2 ½ teaspoons baking powder
- ½ cup granulated sugar
- 8 ounces cold cream cheese
- 1 teaspoon lemon zest, fresh
- 8 tablespoons cold unsalted butter, cut into very small pieces
- 1 organic egg, large
- 6 ounces fresh blueberries
- ¼ cup milk
- 2 teaspoons vanilla extract
- ½ teaspoon salt

For Topping:

- Demerara sugar or sparkling sugar
- Milk

DIRECTIONS

1. Line a large-sized baking sheet with the parchment paper; set aside and then, preheat your oven to 425 F.
2. Whisk the flour with sugar, cornstarch, baking powder & salt in a large-sized mixing bowl. Cut the butter and cream cheese into the flour mixture using a fork or a pastry cutter or even a mixer until you get coarse cornmeal like consistency. Stir in the blueberries and lemon zest; gently toss to combine & set aside until ready to use.
3. Combine the egg with milk and vanilla in a small-sized mixing bowl; whisk well. Pour the wet ingredients into the dry ingredients; give the ingredients a good stir until the dough just begins to hold together; ensure that you don't over mix the ingredients.
4. Sprinkle a work surface with some flour and turn out the dough over it. Fold it over a couple of times until holds together; patting the dough into a ¾" rectangle.
5. Using a round biscuit cutter; cut the scones & gather the scraps up; pat into a separate rectangle & cut out the leftover scones. Transfer the scones to the prepared baking sheet (approximately 2" apart).
6. Brush the tops of scones with some milk and then, sprinkle with the sugar.
7. Bake the scones for 5 to 7 minutes and then, turn off your oven; let the scones to bake in the closed oven until browned lightly, for 6 to 8 minutes. Serve hot with some softened butter & your favorite curd or jam.

CLASSIC ENGLISH SCONES

Prep Time: 20 minutes

Cooking Time: 20 minutes

Servings: 8 persons

INGREDIENTS

- ¾ pound self-rising flour (approximately 2 cups & 13 tablespoons)
- 1 teaspoon baking powder
- 3 ounces cubed butter
- 1 beaten egg, large, to glaze
- 3 tablespoons regular or caster sugar
- 1 teaspoon vanilla extract
- ¾ cup milk
- 1 cup raisins, approximately ½ pound
- A squeeze of lemon juice, fresh
- ¼ teaspoon salt

DIRECTIONS

1. Preheat your oven to 425 F and preheat your baking tray as well.
2. Add the sifted flour with baking powder and salt in a large-sized mixing bowl; mix well.
3. Add the butter; rub in using your fingers until you get fine crumbs like mixture. Next, stir in the sugar using a flat bladed knife and then, add the dried fruit.
4. Put the milk into a jug; heat in the microwave until warm, for 30 seconds or so, but ensure it's not hot. Add the lemon juice and vanilla; set the mixture aside for a minute or two.
5. Make a well in the middle of dry mix and then, add the liquid; quickly combine it using a flat bladed knife. Once done, place it on a work surface, well dusted with the flour; handling the dough as little as possible using soft hands.
6. Take a 2"(5cm) cutter & dip it into some flour. Plunge in a single movement into the dough then, repeat until you get four scones from the dough; press the leftover dough into a round again and then, cut four more pieces from it. When reshaping; it's important for you to use soft hands and be light with the dough; cutting the scone in one vertical action straight down through the dough.
7. Brush the tops with the beaten egg and then, carefully place over the hot baking tray. Bake in the preheated oven until raised & turn golden on the top, for 8 to 10 minutes.

PERFECT CREAM CHEESE PIE CRUST

Prep Time: 20 minutes

Cooking Time: 20 minutes

Servings: 48 persons

INGREDIENTS

- 6 cups all-purpose flour
- 1 package softened cream cheese, (approximately 8 ounce)
- 2 cups softened butter, at room temperature
- A pinch of kosher salt

DIRECTIONS

1. Cream the cream cheese together with butter & salt in a large-sized mixing bowl for a couple of minutes, until blended evenly. Slowly mix in the flour; mix well after each addition until a dough forms; evenly dividing the formed dough into six balls. Use immediately or tightly wrap & freeze until ready to use.

APPLE CREAM PIE

Prep Time: 20 minutes

Cooking Time: 45 minutes

Servings: 8 persons

INGREDIENTS

- 1 pastry shell, unbaked (9")
- 4 cups tart apples, peeled & sliced
- 1 cup heavy whipping cream
- 3 tablespoons all-purpose flour
- 1 cup sugar
- Ground cinnamon

DIRECTIONS

1. Place the apples in pastry shell. Combine flour with sugar & cream in a large-sized mixing until completely smooth; pour on top of the apples and then, sprinkle with the cinnamon.
2. Bake for 8 to 10 minutes, at 400 F. Decrease the heat of your oven to 375 F & continue to bake until the middle is almost set, for 35 to 40 more minutes. To prevent overbrowning; don't forget to cover the edges with aluminum foil during the last 15 minutes of your cooking. Once done; let cool on a wire rack for a couple of minutes. Serve warm or cold.

PEACH GALETTE

Prep Time: 1 hour & 20 minutes

Cooking Time: 20 minutes

Servings: 8 persons

INGREDIENTS

For Crust:

- 1 ¼ cup flour
- 4 ounces (approximately 8 tablespoons, ½ cup) butter, cut into small (½") cubes, chilled in freezer for an hour
- 1 ½ teaspoons sugar
- 4 to 6 tablespoons ice water
- ½ teaspoon salt

For Filling:

- 1 organic egg, large
- 3 tablespoons sugar
- 1 teaspoon butter
- 2 large, not-overly-ripe yellow peaches (approximately ¾ pound), pitted & sliced into ¼" to ½" slices
- 1 tablespoon flour
- ½ teaspoon vanilla extract
- 1 tablespoon of almond paste, optional
- A sprinkling of coarse sugar, optional

DIRECTIONS

1. For the Dough: Pulse the flour with sugar & salt in a food processor until mixed well, for a minute or two. Add the cubed butter & continue to pulse for 8 more times, 10 to 15 seconds increments. Ensure that the butter is still the size of peas in the mixture.
2. Slowly add the ice water; continue to pulse after each addition, until the dough just starts to clump.
3. Turn the dough onto a clean surface and then, form into a disc using clean hands; ensure that you don't over-knead the dough.
4. Sprinkle all sides of the formed dough disk with a small amount of flour. Using a plastic wrap; cover & place in a refrigerator to chill for an hour.
5. Toss the peaches with vanilla, flour & sugar until coated well. Position the rack in the center of your oven and then, preheat it to 425 F. Place the peach slices in a large-sized mixing bowl and sprinkle with the sugar and flour. Gently toss to coat. Sprinkle with the vanilla extract.
6. Next, whisk the egg in a small-sized mixing bowl until completely smooth; set aside until ready to use.
7. Roll the dough out to approximately a 12" diameter on a lightly floured, clean & smooth surface. Gently lift up the rolled-out dough & place it on a rimmed baking sheet.
8. Dot with the almond paste; arrange the peach slices on dough round
9. Arrange the peach slices in a single layer in an overlapping pattern in the middle of your dough; forming approximately a 7 or 8" circle. Dot with a small amount of more butter.
10. Fold the outer edges of the dough round over the filling in an accordion fashion, by approximately 2" all the way around.

11. Coat the exposed dough with the egg wash using a pastry brush and then, sprinkle with the coarse sugar.

12. Place in the preheated oven & bake until nicely browned, for 15 to 20 minutes. Remove from the oven; set aside and let cool over a rack (on the baking sheet) for 12 to 15 minutes. Served with some vanilla ice cream and enjoy.

SOUR CHERRY PIE

Prep Time: 25 minutes

Cooking Time: 1 hour & 20 minutes

Servings: 8 persons

INGREDIENTS

- 1 ¾ cups plus 2 tablespoons all-purpose flour, more for rolling out the dough
- 1 cup sugar
- 2 to 3 tablespoons instant tapioca
- 1 tablespoon brandy or kirsch
- 6 cups sour cherries (approximately 2 pounds), rinsed & pitted
- ¼ teaspoon cinnamon
- 3 tablespoons heavy cream
- Light brown sugar, for sprinkling
- 15 tablespoons unsalted butter, chilled & cut into pieces
- ⅜ teaspoon kosher salt

DIRECTIONS

1. For Dough: Pulse the flour with salt in the bowl of a food processor until just combined. Add butter & continue to pulse for a couple of seconds, until chickpea-size pieces form. Slowly add 3 to 6 tablespoons of ice water & continue to pulse (it's important that you pulse after each addition) until the mixture just comes together. Next, separate the prepared dough into two disks, one with ⅔ of the dough & the other one using the leftover dough. Using a plastic wrap; cover the disks & refrigerate for an hour before rolling out & baking.

2. Next, preheat your oven to 425 F. Place the larger dough disk on a lightly floured surface & roll into a 12" circle, approximately 3/8" thick. Transfer to a 9" pie plate. Line the dough with aluminum foil & weigh it down with the pie weights. Bake in the preheated oven for 25 to 30 minutes, until the crust turns light golden brown.

3. In the meantime, prepare the filling. Combine the sugar with cinnamon and tapioca in bowl of a food processor. Run the motor until tapioca is finely ground. Place the cherries in a large-sized mixing bowl & add the sugar with the prepared tapioca mixture. Drizzle in brandy or kirsch; gently toss until just combined.

4. When the pie crust is ready, immediately transfer it to a wire rack to slightly cool & decrease the heat of

your oven to 375 F. Get rid of the weights & foil; scrapping the cherry filling into the pie crust.

5. Next, place smaller disk of the dough on a lightly floured surface & roll it approximately 3/8" thick; form circles from the dough using a round cookie cutter. Arrange the circles over the cherry filling in your favorite pattern.

6. Brush the top crust with cream & then generously sprinkle with the light brown sugar. Bake for 50 to 55 minutes, until filling begins to bubble, and crust is dark golden brown. Transfer the pie to a wire rack to cool for a couple of hours; let the filling to set before you serve.

LEMON MERINGUE PIE

Prep Time: 2 minutes

Cooking Time: 2 minutes

Servings: 10 persons

INGREDIENTS

- ¾ pound sweet short crust pastry

For Lemon Curd:

- 3 tablespoons unsalted butter

- 6 lemons plus the zest

- 1 ½ cup caster sugar

- 6 whole eggs

For Meringue:

- 1 ⅔ cups caster sugar

- 6 egg whites

DIRECTIONS

1. Roll the sweet short crust pastry out and then, gently wrap it around the rolling pin; line the pastry in a deep tart ring (lightly greased) or a ceramic tourtière dish.

2. Get rid of the pastry excess.

3. Place a sheet of greaseproof paper on the pastry & then, place the baking beans over the top.

4. Blind bake the pastry shell

5. Zest the lemons on top of the sugar and then, squeeze the lemons

6. Next, combine the zest with lemon juice, caster sugar and the whole eggs over low heat in a saucepan; cook for a couple of minutes (ensure that you don't bring it to a boil), stirring frequently with a whisk. Continue to cook until thicken & form a smooth cream (keep an eye on the heat; feel free to adjust it).

7. When almost done; add the butter cubes

8. When the pastry shell is cooked, immediately remove it from the oven & remove the greaseproof paper and baking beans.

9. Pour the lemon preparation into the pastry shell. Evenly spread with a spatula.

10. Bake in the oven to 260 F for 12 to 15 minutes. When done, remove from the oven & leave it to cool. Whip up the egg whites until stiff.

11. Add the caster sugar & continue to whisk for 5 more minutes on high speed.

12. When the meringue is ready; scoop into a piping bag attached with a large fluted nozzle.

13. Pipe swirls of the meringue over lemon preparation.

14. Begin on the outer edge and then work inwards, so that the meringue swirls cover the whole surface of the tart.

15. Brown the meringue using a blow torch or under a hot grill in a hot oven. Set aside in the fridge until ready to serve.

KEY LIME PIE

Prep Time: 20 minutes
Cooking Time: 20 minutes
Servings: 8 persons
INGREDIENTS

- 5 beaten egg yolks, large
- 1 prepared graham cracker crust (9")
- ½ cup key lime juice
- 1 can sweetened condensed milk (14 ounce)

DIRECTIONS

1. Preheat your oven to 375 F.

2. Combine the sweetened condensed milk with lime juice and egg yolks; mix well. Pour into graham cracker shell, unbaked.

3. Bake for 12 to 15 minutes; let cool. Top with the whipped topping & then, garnish with the lime slices.

FRENCH ORANGE CREAM TART

Prep Time: 20 minutes
Cooking Time: 50 minutes
Servings: 8 persons
INGREDIENTS

For Pastry:

- 7 tablespoons cold butter
- ½ teaspoon salt
- 2 tablespoons granulated sugar
- 1 ¼ cups all-purpose flour

- 3 tablespoons cold water

For Orange Filling:

- 2 large eggs
- ⅔ cup granulated sugar
- 8 tablespoons butter
- ⅔ cup fresh orange juice
- 3 egg yolks
- ¼ cup crème fraiche or sour cream
- 4 teaspoons orange zest

DIRECTIONS

1. Combine the flour with sugar & salt in a small-sized mixing bowl.
2. Cut the chilled butter into the flour using a pastry cutter until you get coarse sand like consistency with some pea-sized pieces of the butter. Sprinkle cold water over the prepared mixture & gently toss a couple of times until it just forms a ball that holds together.
3. Separate the dough into two balls; slightly flatten into thick disk shapes. Using a plastic wrap; cover & let chill for a couple of hours.
4. Preheat your oven to 375 F. Roll & trim the dough to form a large circle (enough to fit a 10" fluted tart pan). Fit the circle into the bottom & up the sides of your pan. Line the dough with dried beans or pie weights & bake in the preheated oven for 12 to 15 minutes. Remove the dried beans & bake the shell for 5 more minutes; set the pastry shell aside to cool down (in the tart pan).
5. Stir 8 tablespoons of butter with the crème fraiche in a double boiler. Once combined thoroughly, set the mixture aside.
6. Whisk the eggs with egg yolks & sugar in a separate pan set over the double boiler. Stir the orange juice into the mixture & cook for 2 to 3 minutes, stirring constantly. Add the butter-crème fraiche mixture and orange zest to the eggs & continue to cook for 3 more minutes, stirring constantly.
7. Pour the orange filling into the prepared pastry & bake until turns golden brown & the filling is just set, for 25 to 30 minutes.
8. Let cool on a wire rack in the pan for 12 to 15 minutes. Place in a refrigerator and let chill. Serve chilled & enjoy.

CHOCOLATE PECAN PIE

Prep Time: 20 minutes

Cooking Time: 3 hours & 20 minutes

Servings: 8 persons

INGREDIENTS

For Flaky Pastry:

- 1 cup all-purpose flour
- ⅓ cup lard or ⅓ cup plus 1 tablespoon shortening
- 2 to 3 tablespoons cold water
- ¼ teaspoon salt

For Pecan Filling:

- 1 cup corn syrup
- ⅓ cup margarine or butter, melted
- 2 tablespoons bourbon
- 1 cup pecan broken or halves pecans
- ⅔ cup sugar
- 3 organic eggs, large
- 1 bag semisweet chocolate chips (6 ounces)
- ½ teaspoon salt

DIRECTIONS

1. Preheat your oven to 375 F.
2. Combine the flour with ¼ teaspoon of salt in a medium-sized mixing bowl. Cut in the shortening, using crisscrossing knives or pastry blender, until you get small peas sized particles. Slowly sprinkle with the cold water, tossing with fork until the pastry almost leaves side of bowl & entire flour is moistened.
3. Gather the pastry into a ball; shape into flattened round on lightly floured surface. Roll the pastry into circle (2" larger than the upside-down pie plate, approximately 9x1 ¼") using floured rolling pin. Fold the pastry into ¼ and then, place in the pie plate. Unfold & ease into plate, firmly pressing against the side and bottom. Trim the overhanging edge of pastry approximately 1" from the rim of your pie plate. Fold & roll the pastry under, even with plate; flute per your likings.
4. Next, beat the sugar with bourbon, corn syrup, butter, eggs and ½ teaspoon salt using a hand beater in a large bowl. Stir in the chocolate chips & pecans. Pour into the pastry-lined pie plate. To prevent excess browning; don't forget to cover the edge with 2 to 3" strip of foil. During the last 15 minutes of your baking process; remove the foil.
5. Bake the pie until set, for 45 to 50 minutes. Let cool for half an hour. Refrigerate until chilled, for two more hours.

MONKEY DUNKEY BREAD

Prep Time: 20 minutes

Cooking Time: 40 minutes

Servings: 8 persons

INGREDIENTS

- 3 cans of buttermilk biscuits, Non-flaky; cut each biscuit into quarters

- ½ cup brown sugar
- 2 to 3 teaspoons cinnamon
- 1 cup sugar, light or dark brown
- 2 sticks of butter

DIRECTIONS

1. Preheat your oven to 350 F.
2. Combine the cinnamon with white sugar. Dump these into a 1-gallon zip bag & shake well until evenly mixed.
3. Drop all of the biscuit quarters into the cinnamon-sugar mix. Once done; seal the bag & vigorously shake the ingredients. Evenly spread these nuggets in the bundt pan.
4. Next, over medium-high heat in a saucepan; heat the butter with ½ cup of brown sugar. Cook for a couple of minutes, until you get one color. Once done, pour it on top of the biscuits.
5. Bake in the preheated oven until the crust is a deep dark brown on top, for 30 to 40 minutes. When done, remove them from the oven and then, turn them out on a large plate.

WHITE CHOCOLATE CLUB MED BREAD

Prep Time: 20 minutes

Cooking Time: 1 hour & 50 minutes

Servings: 24 persons

INGREDIENTS

- 4 cups flour
- 2 cups water
- 1 ½ teaspoons gluten
- 2 teaspoons yeast
- 12 ounces white chocolate chips
- 1 ½ teaspoons salt

DIRECTIONS

1. Place flour with gluten and yeast in a large-sized mixing bowl. Mix for a minute with the hook attachment, on medium to low speed.
2. Add water & continue to mix the ingredients for 2 more minutes.
3. Add salt & mix on medium speed for 8 to 10 minutes.
4. Add the chips; continue to mix until the chips are distributed well throughout the dough, for 2 more minutes.
5. Remove the dough from the bowl & kneed lightly into a ball.

6. Put the dough into an oiled bowl. Using a plastic wrap; cover & let rise for 40 to 45 minutes.

7. Cut the dough into two portions and knead them into the desired form; placing them into your pans (lined with silpat or parchment).

8. Let the loaves to rise for an hour and then, bake for 15 to 20 minutes.

CHALLAH WITH RAISIN

Prep Time: 20 minutes

Cooking Time: 2 hours & 50 minutes

Servings: 50 persons

INGREDIENTS

For Dough:

- 1 ¼ cups sugar
- 5 ½ cups warm water or as required
- 2 large eggs plus 2 egg yolks
- 5 ½ pounds high-gluten flour
- 4 tablespoons dry yeast
- 1 cup oil
- 4 tablespoons kosher salt
- ½ cup light sweet raisins

For Egg wash:

- 1 egg yolk
- 1 teaspoon vanilla sugar
- 1 tablespoon water

For Streusel Topping:

- 1 cup flour
- 6 to 7 tablespoons soy-free margarine
- 1 cup sugar

DIRECTIONS

For Dough:

1. Place the sugar with yeast & half of the warm water in the bowl of an electric mixer. Let the yeast to proof for several minutes.

2. Add the flour, eggs, oil & leftover water; alternating the wet & dry ingredients as you add. Add the kosher salt as a dough starts to form; knead for 7 to 8 minutes, on medium speed.

3. Add the raisins; continue to knead until just incorporated, for a more minute, on low speed.

4. Place one teaspoon of oil in the middle of a large bowl. Transfer the formed dough into the bowl; carefully flip until completely coated with the oil. Place the bowl in a large garbage bag & loosely knot

the bag. Let the dough to rise for an hour.

Shape and Bake:

1. Take challah; discarding the challah piece per your minhag. Form the leftover dough into your desired shapes.

2. Combine the entire egg wash ingredients together in a large bowl & brush it on the dough. Let rise for 50 minutes to an hour. In the meantime, preheat your oven to 375 F.

3. Bake the smaller individual challahs for 20 to 25 minutes & large challahs for 40 to 45 minutes.

SUGAR ROSE BRIOCHE

Prep Time: 2 minutes

Cooking Time: 2 minutes

Servings: 8 persons

INGREDIENTS

- 2 cups unbleached all-purpose flour, plus more for dusting work surface
- ¼ cup who le milk
- 2 ¼ teaspoon active dry yeast (approximately 1 packet)
- ½ cup salted butter , softened, cubed, plus more for the tins and the top
- 2 large eggs , plus 1 egg beaten for the egg wash
- ½ cup pralines roses, plus more for top
- 3 tablespoon granulated sugar, plus more for the top
- 1 teaspoon table salt

DIRECTIONS

1. Heat the milk until warm, but ensure that it's not too hot. Add the active dry yeast into the milk; gently stir the ingredients and let for a couple of minutes.

2. Meanwhile, combine the sugar with flour in the bowl of a stand mixer. Add the eggs & beat well.

3. Pour in the milk-yeast mixture; continue to mix the ingredients until you get shaggy dough like consistency. Add butter to the dough & mix well for a couple of minutes, until you get wet, sticky dough like consistency.

4. Scrape the dough from the bowl; turning it out onto a well-floured surface. Knead the dough until smooth compact ball is formed. Place the dough in a clean bowl & cover with a sheet of plastic wrap. Turn on the oven's warm setting for half a minute and then, turn it off. Place the dough in the oven & let rest until almost doubled in size, for 2 hours.

5. Turn out the dough onto a floured surface and then, add approximately ½ cup of the pralines all over the top of the dough. Then fold the sides of the dough inward and over the pralines to envelope the pralines inside the dough. Knead the dough for a bit to help distribute the pralines all throughout the dough.

6. Evenly divide the dough into 8 pieces; rolling each piece into a ball & place them in buttered brioche

tins. Using a plastic wrap; cover the brioche balls & let rise for an hour.

7. Preheat your oven to 375 F. Gently place some of the pralines into the tops of the brioche balls. Brush the tops with the beaten egg & bake until the tops turn deep golden brown, for 16 to 18 minutes. When done; remove the brioche balls from the oven & brush the tops with a mixture of 1 tablespoon sugar and 2 tablespoons melted butter.

BANANA NUT BREAD

Prep Time: 20 minutes

Cooking Time: 1 hour & 20 minutes

Servings: 16 persons

INGREDIENTS

- 2 cups all-purpose flour
- 1 teaspoon rum or vanilla extract
- 2 organic eggs, large
- 1 teaspoon baking soda
- ½ cup softened butter, at room temperature
- 2 tablespoons 2% milk
- 1 ½ cups sugar
- ¾ cup pecans, chopped
- 1 cup ripe bananas, mashed (approximately 2 to 3 medium)
- ½ teaspoon salt

DIRECTIONS

1. Preheat your oven to 325 F. Cream the butter with sugar in a large-sized mixing bowl until light & fluffy, for a couple of minutes. Slowly add the eggs; beat well after each addition and then, beat in the vanilla and milk. Whisk flour with baking soda & salt, in a separate bowl; add to the creamed mixture alternately with the bananas; beat well after each addition and then, fold in the pecans.

   Transfer to a lightly greased 9x5" loaf pan & bake in the preheated oven until a toothpick comes out clean, for 65 to 75 minutes. Let cool in the pan for 10 minutes and then, remove to a wire rack to completely cool.

www.ingramcontent.com/pod-product-compliance
Lightning Source LLC
Chambersburg PA
CBHW081318150726
48001CB00020B/2752